Leveraging
Artificial
Intelligence
for Business Success

Vishal Singhal

INDIA · SINGAPORE · MALAYSIA

Notion Press

No.8, 3rd Cross Street
CIT Colony, Mylapore
Chennai, Tamil Nadu – 600004

First Published by Notion Press 2020
Copyright © Vishal Singhal 2020
All Rights Reserved.

ISBN 978-1-64899-699-3

Dedicated to my Grand Parents

Contents

Preface

'Artificial Intelligence led enterprise' is gaining relevance and becoming mainstream. **"How should we use Artificial Intelligence?"** has become a common question among all management folks and board members of both small and medium companies besides large companies who have already started strategizing on top levels and putting in enormous funds for overall enterprise transformation.

Artificial Intelligence (AI) is considered an integral part of the Fourth Industrial Revolution*. Executives view AI as a key disruptive technology, employees fear it as a job snatcher, consultants pitch it as a cure-all, and the media – hypes and derides it endlessly.

While many large organisations have created strategies and are putting large number of resources to do end-to-end transformation, small and medium companies are still struggling to understand **what it will take to develop AI capabilities in their businesses?** This book tries to address these very concerns and makes it simpler for all (the technical or the non-technical, the initiated or the un-initiated) to understand, what all it will take to make their AI adoption journey* hurdle-free and painless.

The *first chapter* explains why this book, what it covers, and for whom it is intended.

In *second chapter*, author progresses to discuss the inter-relationship of AI, ML, DL, and DS, current state of affairs in AI domain, where the current enterprise stands around the world and what kinds of tasks are automatable by AI. It also deals with the reasons, benefits, various tasks helped, barriers, and challenges faced by companies in adopting AI and ends with how AI would probably impact the workforce.

In AI domain, most critical components are talent and data. Talent is hard to find, hire and retain so *third chapter* deals with what all kinds of talent is required in an enterprise if one wants to set up a team for AI initiatives.

Data, being the other key component, is dealt in the *fourth chapter* elaborating the challenges faced by companies in collecting the data, types of data-sets, errors that should be avoided in order to have right quantity and quality of data-sets and finally talks about factors that should be kept in mind so monetisation* can be built into the data right upfront before it's used in training the machines.

All enterprise-heads face this dilemma – 'where to start their AI initiatives?' Many companies worldwide which have adopted AI, say that their revenues increased while many others say AI helped them in reducing costs. Overall, executives say, 13 trillion worth of GDP growth is expected by 2030 just due to AI which will mainly come from sectors like manufacturing, agriculture, energy, logistics, and education. Hence, the *fifth chapter* discusses various use cases in areas like retail, human resources, finance, sales, and social domains. The chapter concludes in describing steps on setting up your AI project for success.

Post-selection of areas where AI can be deployed, executives feel the next dilemma of 'whether to build, buy or outsource the AI deployment?', considering that there is so much to do and if they miss certain steps or don't have anybody to benchmark it against, then the project may fall flat. So, the *sixth chapter* discusses about the best ways an enterprise can deploy artificial intelligence in order that confidence comes in executives' minds about the success of the same and it can be pursued further from there.

The *seventh chapter* deals with the rise of internal AI labs which can play a crucial role in developing AI focussed and AI educated workforce in small and medium enterprises/businesses in an effective way.

Last but one chapter (that is the *eighth*) discusses the potential pitfalls and errors/mistakes that should be avoided to make the AI initiatives successful. It talks about the burning topics like explainable-AI, ethics, bias, security and many more.

The author concludes this book in *chapter ninth* by letting Artificial Intelligence generate the future it sees that is in store for humans to see.

It may be pointed out here that the data shared by author in the whole book is derived from various international research organisations and most of it relates to large companies worldwide whereas only meagre data on small/medium company is available to be listed as most of these companies are still to adopt and exploit AI technologies before their data is collected by these research organisations. Thus, the given data of these research reports more or less applies to small/medium enterprises and will continue to do so till similarly relevant data related to SMEs/SBEs starts appearing.

The wise reader will take cognizance of the fact that as the AI field is growing and expanding at a rapid pace and influencing human life in a myriad ways, no book like the one in your hands can claim to represent the complete scenario at any given time. One has to keep oneself abreast with the dynamic growth of AI and its applications through various sources, if one wants to remain updated and take best advantage out of it. However, the author reasonably believes and trusts that this book will equip its readers with ample information, basic concepts as well as dynamics of AI and lay firm ground to build their own castles upon it.

Moreover, for readers' ease of understanding, a **glossary** has been included in the end of the book to refer any difficult-to-understand words/ technical terms, etc. and the same has been marked by asterix (*) in respective places in the text for an indication. Similarly, a list of

references and a subject **index** have been added thereafter, for quick referencing.

Although most of the references of figures etc., incorporated in the text, have been mentioned appropriately, a few might have been left due to our not being able to locate accurately or left inadvertently. This lacuna is sincerely regretted.

The author looks forward for receiving constructive criticism from its elite readers so that the same could be incorporated appropriately to enhance the usefulness of the book in its next edition.

Vishal Singhal

(Author)

Acknowledgements

I would like to thank following contributors without whose invaluable support, this book would not have been possible:

- My friend Vikas Jain (Speaker & Founder, The Real Education. com) who inspired me to write the book without procrastination and guided me on criticalities at various stages of writing the book.

- My endearing parents for constant inspiration and guidance to write the book.

- Bhavesh Laddagiri (youngest member in CellStrat AI Lab and a deep learning researcher) for all illustrations in the book and helping in the concluding chapter generation through artificial intelligence itself.

- My wife Ritu to keep pushing me to complete the book.

- My son Vihan (fifth std.) to motivate me early morning to work hard to achieve my goal.

- My elder brother Vivek, co-founder CellStrat (a research oriented Artificial Intelligence focussed e-learning company) for being constant critique and motivating me to do better.

- Mr. Arun Gupta, Founder – Synergy Education and Research Society, my senior friend and guide, for his invaluable inputs and guidance in the language and compilation of the book.

- My mentor Prof. M. M. Pant (a senior academic research & management professional, now promoter of alternative forms of pedagogy and First Pro-Vice Chancellor of IGNOU) for agreeing to write the foreword for the book.

- My Publisher – Notion Press for publishing my book under their name.

Author

Foreword

One may wonder if there is a need for yet another book on Artificial Intelligence. But after going through this interesting, informative, and engaging book by Vishal Singhal, one would be convinced that this book is indeed very useful.

The book is reasonably short in its length with about 152 pages, but for its compactness it is quite comprehensive. It is structured as 9 chapters (other than chapter 1 which touches upon the *raison d'etre* for the book) and addresses issues of major concerns of practitioners.

Chapter 1 articulates the reasons for writing the book and identifies the persona of the reader. One of the challenges that I have found amongst even people and organisations enthusiastic about starting their AI explorations is where to begin. Many believe that learning a programming language like Python is the starting point. Worse still, many get lost in the labyrinths of the mathematics of the wide variety of algorithms, which eventually intimidates them into giving up. Some get so swayed by the lack of 'explainability of AI' that they give up. Chapter 5 of the book responds very lucidly to this challenge of where and how to begin? It also shares the characteristics of a good AI pilot project.

One of the interesting topics in the book is on Data Fallacies in the chapter on data. Thirteen types of data fallacies are explained in the book. Some of these like the 'false causality' are the traditional logical fallacy of *ergo hoc propter hoc.*

Most businesses will in due course move on to 'Social Commerce', and to successfully leverage Social Commerce*, the deployment of Artificial Intelligence and Machine Learning is a *sine qua non.*

To me the biggest impact of this book will be that it will encourage a large number of what are traditionally labelled small and medium enterprises to venture into the uncharted territories of Artificial Intelligence and Machine Learning. And when they grow into successful entities, they will fondly remember Vishal Singhal and this book as their breakthrough motivators that changed their life's trajectory.

My best wishes for success to the author and all his readers.

Prof. M. M. Pant
Former Pro Vice-Chancellor IGNOU

Motive Behind this Book

Why this book?

Artificial Intelligence* (AI) is considered an integral part of the Fourth Industrial Revolution*. Executives view AI as a key disruptive technology*, employee fear it as a job destroyer, consultants pitch it as a cure-all, and the media – hypes and derides it endlessly. Its impact, and far-reaching consequences, while acknowledged, are yet to be comprehended in their entirety by all.

Business Organisations using AI most aggressively are large business houses with the most data — online platforms, financial services, telecommunications, and retail. While small-to-medium-sized enterprises, business-to-business firms, and those in basic manufacturing industries though want to but are less likely to use AI. Business establishments outside the United States are also pursuing AI but at a slower pace, although there exist aggressive adopters in China, the U.K., Canada, and Singapore. Regulatory agencies and governments across the globe are formulating national policies and laws around this technology to protect the rights of the digital citizens, as well as to empower them. Even private, non-profit organizations are also contributing to democratize the technology by making it accessible and affordable.

The author has spoken in multiple conferences, seminars, workshops and webinars. Everywhere, he has faced this question umpteen times from all sorts of audience, right from – students to teachers to employees in small, medium and large companies to entrepreneurs of all sizes and types (proprietors, firms, companies, etc.) - **How can we deploy and benefit from Artificial Intelligence?**

Honestly, there is no short, simple, straight-forward, one-size-fit-all answer to this question. AI deployment* will vary vastly from one type to other and one size company to other.

This book endeavours to answer the above question as precisely as possible for the benefit of all concerned.

What this book covers?

This book covers topics (in chapters) like the current big picture, skills/ capabilities needed for AI deployment, data types, finding a starting point, AI enabling ways, precautions, conclusions, and internal AI labs. These chapters further deal with sub-topics like reasons for opting AI adoption, pace, impact on workforce, barriers etc. besides skill-sets, data fallacies*, areas where AI can be deployed, uses of AI currently in vogue, ways in which AI acts as an enabler, potential pitfalls to be avoided and future projections.

For whom this book is intended?

This book can be useful for a wide variety of readers, but has been written with two main target groups in mind, one group includes the business owners, the self-employed people, home based small office people, small and medium enterprises or large-scale companies learning about AI field to benefit from it as an enterprise enabler and the other target group includes professionals working in these companies. Though the book relates to AI, yet is not that technical, does not involve any coding or programming examples or references and is ideally meant for management and strategy professionals as well as CXO suite who would like to transform their businesses for better.

To better comprehend how AI will impact your company's situation, consider three questions as you read:

Q.1 Which AI technologies may have the greatest potential benefit to your organization?

Q.2 How might those technologies enable new strategies, business models, or business process designs?

Q.3 How do you anticipate, AI will impact your workforce, and how can you begin to prepare employees to augment AI capabilities?

This book tries to cover all possible steps in AI deployment and enablement, but all steps may not be applicable to all the companies/ entities depending on the stage of business they are in as well as the size of their businesses. 'Simply asking the questions' shall be the first step in starting your company up the path of transformation.

2 *Chapter*

Understanding the Big Picture

The most important general-purpose technology of our era is Artificial Intelligence (AI), particularly Machine Learning* (ML)—that is, the machine's ability to keep improving its performance without humans having to explain exactly how to accomplish all the tasks it's given. Recently, within just few years, machine learning has become far more effective and widely available. Experts can now build systems that learn how to perform tasks on their own.

Advance form of Machine Learning is called Deep Learning* and Data Science* is the backbone of AI and Machine Learning. Relationship of all these is summarised in figure 2.1 below:

The extent of AI will be magnified in the coming decade, as almost every sector (manufacturing, retail, law, insurance, education, transport, finance, health care, advertising, entertainment, and virtually every other industry) transforms its core processes and business models to take advantage of artificial intelligence. The bottleneck currently felt is in AI imagination, implementation, and management.

However, like so many other new technologies, AI also has generated several unrealistic expectations. For example, simply calling a matrimonial site 'AI-powered,' doesn't make it any more effective, although it may help with fund-raising.

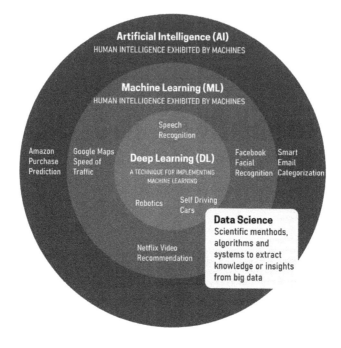

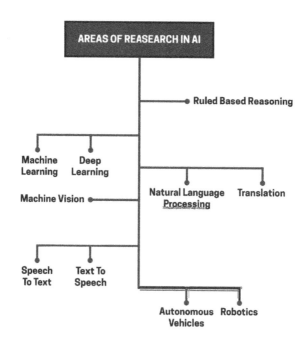

Figure – 2.1

One AI expert wonders, 'these days it has become critical to ascertain whether AI has been built into marketing or company is actually marketing AI solutions'. This chapter attempts to cut through the noise to recognise and describe the real potential of AI, its practical implications, and the barriers to its adoption.

Current Situation of Artificial Intelligence

Artificial Intelligence is spreading to almost all spheres of our lives - be it healthcare, retail, finance or any others. In an enterprise scenario, AI adoption can be summed up as shown in figure 2.2.

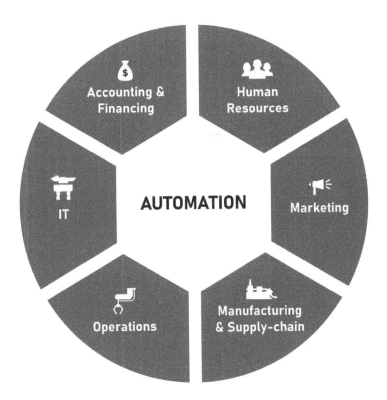

Figure – 2.2

Besides this, what follows is a list that contains some of the most impressive feats of machine intelligence around. And as you can observe, this list is not comprehensive and is continually expanding.

What AI can do?

Everyday Human Stuff

- 👓 Recognize objects in images

- 📖 Navigate the map of a metro underground

- 📞 Transcribe speech better than professional transcribers

- 🌐 Translate between languages

- 😮 Speak

- **?** Pick out the bit of a paragraph that answers your question

- 🙁 Recognize emotions in facial images

- 🐵 Recognise emotions in speech

Travel

- 🚗 Drive

- ☞ Fly a drone

- 🅿 Predict parking difficulty by area

Medical Science

- 💊 Discover new uses for existing drugs

- 🔬 Spot cancer in tissue slides better than human histo-pathologists

- 🔍 Predict hypoglycemic events in diabetics three hours in advance

- 👁 Identify diabetic retinopathy (a leading cause of blindness) from retinal photos

- 🧬 Detect gene sequences (of DNA) to diagnose human genetic disorders

- 📷 Detect a range of medical conditions from patients' images

Science

- Solve the quantum state of many particles at once

Agriculture

- Predict crop yields

- Sort cucumbers

- Detect crop diseases

- Spray pesticide with pinpoint accuracy

Security

- Spot burglars in any premises

- Write its own encryption language

- Predict social unrest 5 days before it happens

- Unscramble pixelated images

- Detect malware

- Verify a person's identity

- Anticipate fraudulent payment attacks before they happen

Finance

- Trade stocks

- Handle insurance claims

Law

- Predict the outcomes of cases at the European Court of Human Rights with 79% accuracy

- Do legal case research

- Do due diligence on Mergers & Acquisitions (M&A) deals

- Flag errors in legal documents

Games & tests

- 🖥 Beat humans at Jeopardy*
- 🎮 Absolutely nail Super Mario*
- 🐵 Play Breakout* like a total professional
- ● Play Go* better than humans

Assistance

- ▦ Schedule meetings by email
- 🏃 Be your personal trainer

Programming

- 🖥 Write software unit tests

Meteorology

- ☁ Identify potentially threatening weather

Creativity

- 🎨 Paint a pretty good van Gogh*
- ✍ Write poems that get published
- 🎼 Write music
- ✎ Design logos
- 🍴 Come up with its own recipes
- 🏈 Write sports articles for the Associated Press
- 🎬 Write film scripts
- ⚽ Play soccer badly
- 🎧 Recommend songs you'll like

Boring but Important

- ⬤ Lip-read better than humans

- ⬛ Optimize energy usage in air-conditioning units in Google's data centres

Full-on Unbelievable Stuff

- ⬤ Become a Twitter troll

- ⬤ Collaborate (or become aggressive)

- ∞ Write its own machine learning software

Why to Adopt Artificial Intelligence?

One may like to learn, why artificial intelligence is being adopted by enterprises worldwide. Figures 2.3 & 2.4 reveal the reasons:

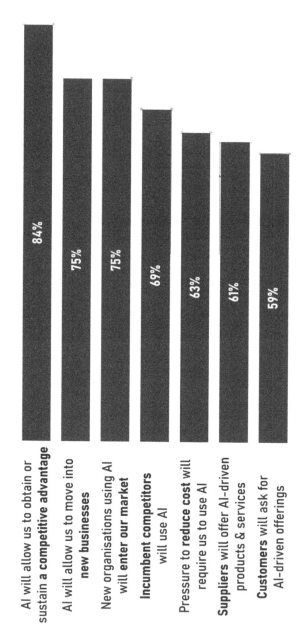

Figure – 2.3

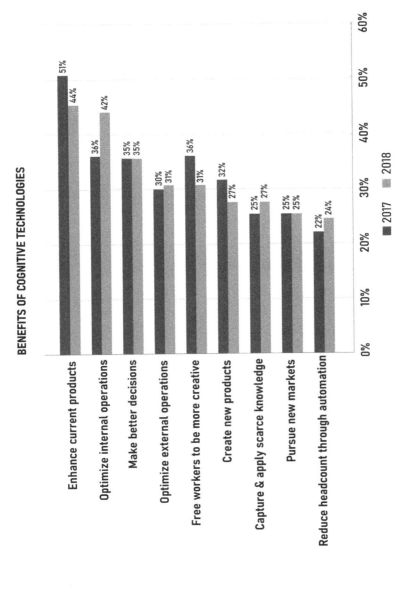

Figure – 2.4

(Source: Deloitte 2018 Cognitive* Survey)

What do Humans Use AI for?

This question comes to mind when one thinks of as to when so much of AI deployment* is happening, what could humans in these organisations be using AI for? To answer this question, Gartner did a research and following results came out (figure 2.5):

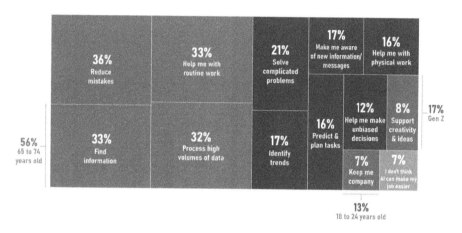

(Source: Gartner)

Figure – 2.5

Top Barriers Inhibiting Companies from adopting Artificial Intelligence

This is a natural question that comes to our mind as to what are the general, most prevalent reasons for not adopting AI by companies worldwide even when reasons for adopting AI are so strong and can benefit the enterprises so profusely. Large enterprises give the following reasons as most prevalent (figure 2.6):

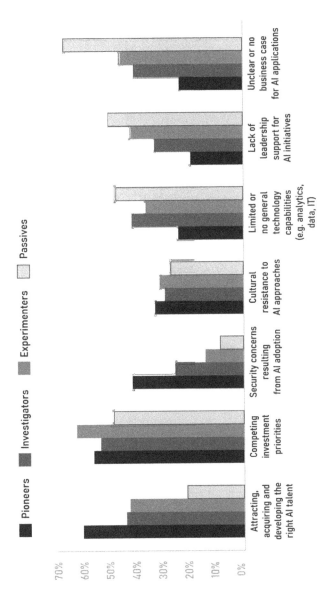

Ref: *MIT Research Report-2017*

Figure – 2.6

Above are the barriers stated by large enterprises. However, small and medium size companies state entirely different reasons as barriers to AI adoption. Broadly, these are ***enterprise maturity, fear of unknown, finding a starting point,*** and ***vendor strategy***. These are also visible in the figure 2.7 below:

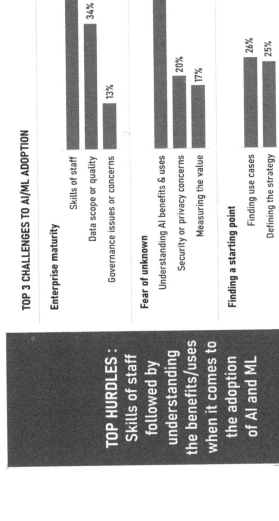

Figure – 2.7

(Source: Gartner)

All the above barriers have been dealt in subsequent chapters.

Probable Impact of Artificial Intelligence Adoption on Workforce

Majority of the workforce believes, if artificial intelligence-based automation happens, it will adversely affect the jobs and thus a considerable manpower will be affected in a negative sense (figure 2.8).

This may be true for large companies. However, for small and medium companies, management/business owners are trying to still assess - how to go about in deploying artificial intelligence technologies? It will enable them to benefit monetarily while maintaining the manpower as well as be able to compete with their competitors, who have already been more efficient and now with AI adoption, they are growing bigger.

This book endeavours to encourage and enable these SMEs* and SBEs* to adopt AI while also helping them compete with their competitors efficiently.

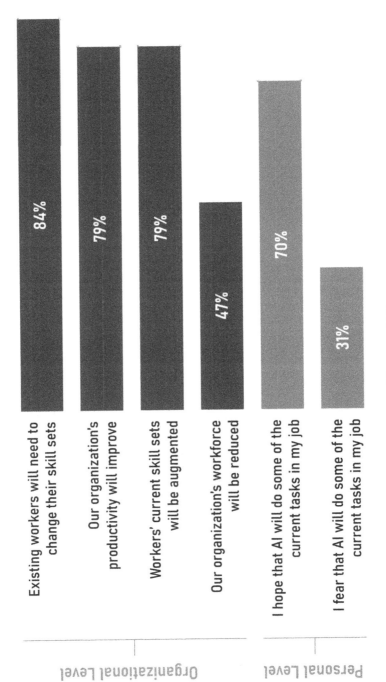

How do you expect AI will affect the workforce in the next five years?

Organizational Level

- Existing workers will need to change their skill sets — 84%
- Our organization's productivity will improve — 79%
- Workers' current skill sets will be augmented — 79%
- Our organization's workforce will be reduced — 47%

Personal Level

- I hope that AI will do some of the current tasks in my job — 70%
- I fear that AI will do some of the current tasks in my job — 31%

Figure – 2.8

Pace of Adoption of Artificial Intelligence

Figure 2.9 shows the adoption status of AI in most developed nations. However, it might be said, it's mostly the case across the board and this slow adoption can be attributed to the barriers discussed above.

Figure – 2.9

(Source: Gartner)

Most companies across the world are still unable to deploy AI, possibly due to lack of 'strategy', 'pathways', and 'suitability of data' required for the effective deployment of the AI technologies.

Skills/Capabilities Needed for Enterprise AI Deployment

Enterprise AI* deployment demands a team comprising of several data-science or AI roles to work on and deliver a data science project. So, let's understand these roles. Each role has its own skills that are critical to data science projects at various stages.

AI/DATA SCIENCE ROLES IN ENTERPRISE AI

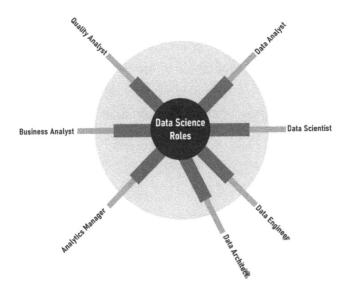

Figure – 3.1

Skill Sets required in an AI Enterprise

Data Analyst

A data analyst* translates numbers into plain English. Each business establishment collects data whether it's sales figures, market research, logistics, or transportation costs. A data analyst's job is to take that data and use it to help the business establishment make better business decisions. There are several different types of data analysts in the field, including operations analysts, marketing analysts and financial analysts, etc.

Data Scientist

A data scientist* is someone who knows how to extract meaning from and interpret data, which requires both tools and methods from Statistics and machine learning. S/he spends a lot of time in the process of collecting, cleaning, and managing data. Domain knowledge is also an integral part of the skill.

Data Engineer

A data engineer* is responsible for the creation and maintenance of analytics infrastructure that enables almost every other function in the data world. S/he is responsible for the development, construction, maintenance, and testing of architectures, such as databases and large-scale processing systems.

Data Architect

A data architect* builds complex computer database systems for companies either for the general public or for individual companies. S/he works with a team that looks at the needs of the database, the data that is available and creates a blueprint for creating, testing and maintaining that data architecture*.

Data Science (DS)/Analytics Manager

A data science*/analytics manager coordinates the different tasks that must be completed by the team for a DS/AI project. Tasks may include researching and creating effective methods to collect data, analysing information and recommending solutions to business.

Data Science (DS) Business Analyst

A data science business analyst converts a business problem statement to a Data Science/AI problem statement which means that data needs to be analysed to arrive at the insights*. The data would then be reviewed with the technology team and results would be delivered to the business team in the form of insights and data patterns. The business analyst should also be skilled enough to apply various predictive modelling techniques and right model selection for generating insights for the problem at hand.

Quality Analyst*

The job of a quality analyst includes checking the quality of the training data-set, preparing them for testing, running Statistics* on human labelled data-sets, evaluating precision and recall on the resulting ML models, reporting on expected patterns in outputs, and implementing necessary tools to automate repetitive parts of the work. Experience in software testing with data quality or DS/ML focus, understanding of Statistics, exposure to data science/machine learning techniques and coding proficiency in Python* (a programming language), are some of the skills required for the job.

In general, companies are advised to hire people from the industry itself instead of from the academia directly as the talent coming from the later source is likely to be more interested in working on paper writing/experimentations and habitual of coming out with brilliant/innovative/imaginative/elegant yet extravagant solution (demanding more resources of the company in terms of time, money, personnel, major changes in setup, etc.) rather than focusing on the current problem and suggesting practical solution befitting the existing problem in the shortest possible time. On the other hand, in the industry working culture, s/he is allowed limited time to come out with analytics solution that just fits the need. However, the management should use their rich experience in evaluating the right fresh talent and hiring them as there are exceptions to every rule.

How Data Scientists spend most of their time?

A natural curiosity may exist among the readers as to how data scientists spend most of their time. Well, percentage wise the job of cleaning and organising data consumes sixty percent of their time. Collecting data set comes next at nineteen percent. Mining data for patterns takes less than ten percent, while building training set, refining algorithms and others take less than five percent each (figure 3.2):

TIME

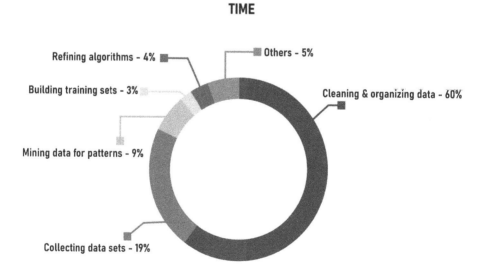

Figure – 3.2

Data - The Key for Successful AI Deployment

Data

Artificial Intelligence depends predominantly on data. It's the most crucial factor that makes system training possible and explains why machine learning became so popular in recent years. But irrespective of enterprise's actual load of information and data science expertise, a machine will nearly be useless or perhaps even harmful if one can't make sense of data records.

It may be stressed here that all data is flawed because at the beginning of adopting the AI journey in an enterprise, it is discovered their data is stored in varied formats over different kinds of databases across systems, as data was not initially collected with the thought of implementing machine learning models. In short, data collection/preparation is a set of procedures that helps make the dataset more suitable for machine learning. In broader terms, the data preparation also includes establishing the right data collection mechanism. And these procedures consume most of the time spent on machine learning. Sometimes it takes months before the first algorithm* is built.

Each project or team has its own style of storing data in the required or preferred systems and formats. If the process of storing data has been manual, many errors in data inputs are highly expected.

All the collected data from which no one can make any relevant inference, is called 'dirty data'. Therefore, in order to be consumable by the data science team, data needs to be collected/ prepared and formatted into a standard format. A good practice to achieve this is to involve a domain expert before standardizing the format of the data. Most of the machine learning algorithms which are in use, require 'clean data'.

Converting data types to the correct intended formats is best before storing on a common system for further use. If the data is not formatted appropriately, it often leads to incorrect analysis and predictions. Formatted data is more clear, easier to aggregate and easier to compare.

Some of the obstacles encountered while converting collected data into a standard format may be the following:

- missing values

- invalid values

- scale of the data

- null values/non consumable data

Let's have a look at ways to solve an enterprise's data problems:

1. How to collect data for AI initiatives of an enterprise that doesn't possess any data?

For those who've just begun their AI initiatives, lack of data is a common problem encountered and expected, but fortunately, there are ways to solve this problem.

- An enterprise has a chance to collect data the right way. The enterprises that started data collection with paper ledgers and ended with .xlsx* and .csv* files are likely to have a harder time with data preparation than those who have a small but AI-friendly dataset.

If you know the tasks that machine learning should solve, you can tailor a data-gathering mechanism in advance. Beginners are suggested to start small & keep the complexity of their data low.

2. Articulate the Problem early:

Knowing 'what an enterprise wants to predict' will help them to decide which data may be more valuable to collect. When formulating the problem, an enterprise should conduct data exploration and try to think in the categories of classification, clustering, regression, and ranking. In layman's language, these tasks are differentiated in the following ways:

Classification: This model attempts to draw some conclusion from the observed values. Given one or more inputs, a classification model will try to predict the value of one or more outcomes. For example, when filtering emails – 'spam' or 'not spam', when looking at transaction data – 'fraudulent' or 'authorized'.

Clustering: You want an algorithm to find the rules of classification and the number of classes. For example, this usually happens when one needs to segment their customers and tailor a specific approach to each segment depending on its characteristics.

Regression: Enterprise wants an algorithm to yield some numeric value. For example, if one spends too much time coming up with the right price for their products since it depends on several factors, regression algorithms can aid in estimating these values.

Ranking: Some machine learning algorithms just rank objects by a number of features. Ranking is actively used to recommend movies in video streaming services or show the products that a customer might purchase with a high probability based on his/ her previous search and purchase activities.

It's likely, that a business problem can be solved within this simple segmentation and enterprise may start adapting the datasets accordingly. The 'rule of thumb' at this stage is to avoid over-complicated problems and thus start small.

3. Establish Data Collection Mechanisms

'Creating a data-driven culture in an enterprise' is perhaps the hardest yet most crucial part of the entire initiative. When AI is used for predictive analytics*, the first thing to do is to tackle data fragmentation. For example, Hotels know their guests' credit card numbers, types of amenities they choose, sometimes home addresses, room service use, and even drinks and meals ordered during a stay. The website where people book these rooms, however, may treat them as complete strangers.

This data gets siloed in different departments and even different tracking points within a department. Marketers may have access to a Customer Relationship Management (CRM)* but the customers there aren't associated with web analytics. It's not always possible to converge all data streams if company has many channels of engagement, acquisition, and retention, but in most cases it's manageable.

Another factor here is the human factor. Data collection may be a dull/ monotonous task that burdens enterprise's employees and overwhelms them with instructions. If people must constantly and manually make records, the probability is, they will consider these tasks as yet another bureaucratic whim and let the job slide. For instance, Salesforce provides a decent toolset to track and analyse activities of salespeople, but manual data entry and activity logging distances salespeople.

4. Data Cleaning

Missing values noticeably reduces prediction accuracy. In terms of machine learning, assumed or approximated values are 'rather right' for an algorithm* than just missing ones. Even if one doesn't know the exact value, methods are there to 'better assume' which value is missing or bypass the issue.

Choosing the right approach for 'How to clean data?' depends largely on the nature of data and the domain or problem at hand, the enterprise is in. Following approaches are suggested:

- Substitute missing values with dummy values, e.g. n/a for categorical or 0 for numerical values.

- Substitute the missing numerical values with mean figures.

- For categorical values, one can also use the most frequent items to fill in.

5. Data Formatting to be made Consistent

Data formatting is sometimes referred to as the 'file format' you're using. And this isn't much of a problem to convert a dataset into a file format that fits your machine learning system best.

Here, format consistency of records itself is being referred. If an enterprise aggregates data from different sources or its dataset has been manually updated by different people, it's worth making sure that all variables within a given attribute are consistently written. These may be date formats (05/07/2000 or July 05, 2000 or 5 July 2000), sums of money (5.03 or Rs./ US\$ 5.03, or even 5 rupees 3 paise/ 5 dollars 3 cents), addresses, etc. The input format(s) should be same across the entire dataset.

And there are other aspects of data consistency. For instance, if you have a set numeric range in an attribute from 0.0 to 5.0, ensure that there are no 5.5s in your set.

6. Desirable Data-Set Types

Datasets are an integral part of the field of machine learning. Datatypes on the other hand vary for various kinds of datasets, used in solving various kinds of problems. Inexperienced executives mostly faulter in this step and collect inappropriate kinds or mixed datasets for solving their problems leading to a waste of time, money, and resources. Following are some of the most popular kinds of datasets required for some popular kinds of problems:

Use Case	Dataset Description	Format
Face Recognition	Clear images of the faces of individuals	Image
Action Recognition	Dataset of video clips containing the specific actions	Videos, .CSV* for labels
Object Detection	Images with corresponding bounding box data with labels	Image, XML*
Object Segmentation	Coloured masks of background, and foreground objects	Images, JSON* (COCO* format)
Handwriting Recognition	Handwritten dataset with bounding box data for each character and the corresponding label	Image, XML
News/Review Classification	Large corpuses of text with corresponding labels	.CSV or text files
Question Answering Systems	Dataset with context, question and answer (answer is a subset of the context)	JSON or .CSV
Information Retrieval (IR) Systems	Text corpus	.CSV or text files
Chatbots	Multiple questions and responses for the same intent.	.CSV or text files

Figure – 4.1

7. Desirable Data-Set Sizes

It is often asked 'What the desirable data-set size is, to start a machine learning model?' – Well, the answer is: It depends upon…

a)   Complexity of the business problem,

b)   Complexity of the algorithm in use, and

c)   Sensitivity of the prediction.

There are two ways to answer the desirable data-set size question:

-   Consult a domain expert.

-   Get all the data you can.

Private & Public Datasets

Private datasets capture the specifics of one's unique business and potentially have all relevant attributes that might be needed for predictions. But the question arises - *when can one use public datasets?*

Public datasets come from business organisations that are open to sharing. These datasets usually contain information about general processes in a wide range of life areas like healthcare records, historical weather records, transportation measurements, text and translation collections, records of hardware use, etc. Though these will not help capture data dependencies in one's business, they can yield great insight into any industry and its niche, and, sometimes, its customer segments.

One can find great public datasets compilation on GitHub*. Some of the public datasets are commercial and can be availed at a cost.

Another use case for public-datasets comes from start-ups and businesses that use machine learning techniques to ship ML-based products to their customers. For example, if a business recommends city attractions and restaurants based on user-generated content, they do not have to label thousands of pictures to train an image recognition algorithm that will sort through photos, sent by users. There is an Open

Images dataset from Google. Similar datasets exist for speech and text recognition too.

So, even if enterprises have not been collecting data for years, they can go ahead and search. There may be sets that they can use right away.

Finally: one still needs a **data scientist/consultant.**

The dataset preparation measures described here are basic and direct. So, one must still find data scientists/consultants and data engineers if they need to automate data collection mechanisms, set the infrastructure, and scale for complex machine learning tasks.

(Ref: Altexsoft.com)

Data Fallacies* to be avoided for Best Results

Artificial Intelligence deployment demands huge data sets relevant to the problem statement. Thus, data collectors are given the responsibility of collecting lots of data in their respective departments. However, many a times they may intentionally or un-intentionally commit some errors while collecting the data which will result in bad results later when AI models are deployed. Thirteen different kinds of such errors, also called fallacies, are given below that must be avoided as much as possible for best results:

Cherry Picking

Figure – 4.2

1. Cherry Picking:

It means selecting those data or results that most favour the situation instead of whole data in its entirety.

This will only show a very rosy picture in modelling but eradicate the unfavourable results thus leading to bad deployment. As when new data comes in comprising of both good and bad data, results will not be so good thus creating bad taste for all.

2. Data Dredging:

It means using same kind of data for all kinds of problems. But this may be, only by chance, that any hypothesis will come out, let alone correct or in-correct. It's like applying human resource related AI models on external customers'

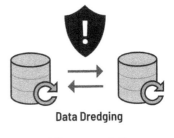

Data Dredging

Figure – 4.3

data instead of internal customers' of company i.e. employees. Thus, results would be bad.

Survivorship Bias

Figure – 4.4

3. Survivorship Bias:

It happens in resulting insights when there is fallacy in data as it has been either cherry picked or have survived some selection criteria initially.

4. Cobra Effect:

It happens when a wrong reward is offered to a machine learning model as an incentive for achieving certain kinds of results. However, being wrong reward, it produces an opposite result than what is intended. This kind of reward is also called Perverse Incentive.

Cobra Effect

Figure – 4.5

False Causality

Figure – 4.6

5. False Causality:

It refers to wrongly interpreting cause of one event due to other. E.g. Heavy Rains/ fires in one-part of the world due to pleasant weather in some other part of the world.

■ Sample
▨ Population

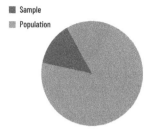

Sampling Bias

Figure - 4.7

6. Sampling Bias:

It happens when for example only dogs, cats and goats' data is collected leaving out sheep and other animals, thus not taking all representatives of the animal kingdom and trying to draw conclusions from this limited population, causes sampling bias.

7. Gambler's Fallacy:

Also known as 'Monte Carlo Fallacy' or the 'Fallacy of the Maturity of Chances', it is an erroneous belief that if a particular event occurs more frequently than normal during the past, it is less likely to happen in the future (or vice versa), when it has otherwise been established that the probability of such events does not depend on what has happened in the past. Such events, having the quality of historical independence, are referred to as 'statistically independent'.

Gambler's Fallacy

Figure – 4.8

The fallacy is commonly associated with gambling, wherein it may be believed, for example, that the next dice roll is more than usually likely to be six because there have recently been less than the usual number of sixes.

8. Hawthorne Effect:

It refers to the fact that when someone keeps a check on them, they tend to perform well. Thus, this is also known as Observer Effect.

Hawthorne Effect

Figure – 4.9

9. Regression towards the Mean:

It refers to the situation when some trend is usually good or bad for some time, it will tend to fall to average position over time. For example, Apple* dominated its number one position for

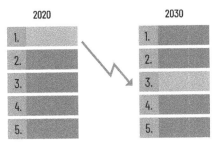

Regression Towards Mean

Figure – 4.10

some time in the global market among its various categories of products but ultimately it slid to lower ranks in those categories.

McNamara Fallacy

Figure – 4.11

10. McNamara Fallacy:

It involves making a decision based solely on quantitative observations (e.g. metrics, statistics etc.) and all other "qualitative" factors based on domain knowledge are ignored.

11. Overfitting:

It is said to happen when, for example, an autonomous car trained on Indian road conditions is driven on American roads will be said to be overfitted for US roads.

12. Publication Bias:

Many a times researchers (to get their research paper

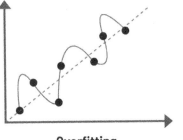

Overfitting

Figure – 4.12

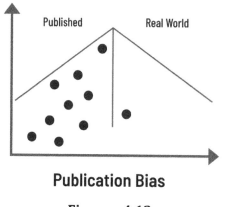

Publication Bias

Figure – 4.13

published) collect their own data in order to be original but also overfit the data or bring in all sorts of above kinds of fallacies in the data and thus the insights generated from it, look good. But this creates distortion among the minds of the reader who refer the same in their studies/ experiments, taking the distorted source as correct. This causes the publication bias to happen.

Dangers of Summary Metrics

Figure – 4.14

13.   Danger   of Summary Metrics:

It refers to looking only at summary metrics and missing big differences in raw data.

E.g.: Assume a business, through its promotions, has increased its number of email subscribers. On the surface, it looks like a great sign, but not necessarily. What if the number of people, who never open their email, increased? Without having the email read, the increased subscriber count would be useless, and measuring the metric blindly could be highly misleading.

Data Monetization Factors

Lot of care needs to be taken while handling data as it may lead to monetisation for the enterprise, if handled correctly.

Following are the data monetisation factors which need to be taken care of, in order to set-up good data handling practice inside the enterprise. These factors determine the success of any analytics initiative to an extent:

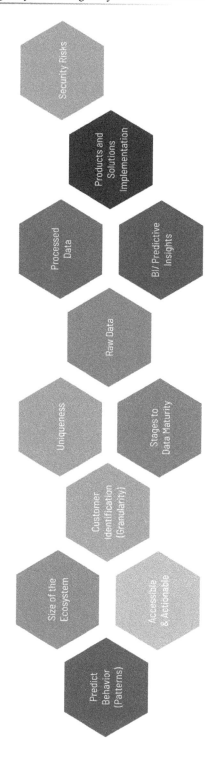

Figure - 4.15

(Ref: AI & Analytics, Wiley | Prediction Machines, HBR)

Predict Behavior (Patterns)

Enterprise data should be detailed enough to build a successful data monetisation strategy. E.g. Customer data should be detailed enough to be able to predict customer behavior, patterns and more.

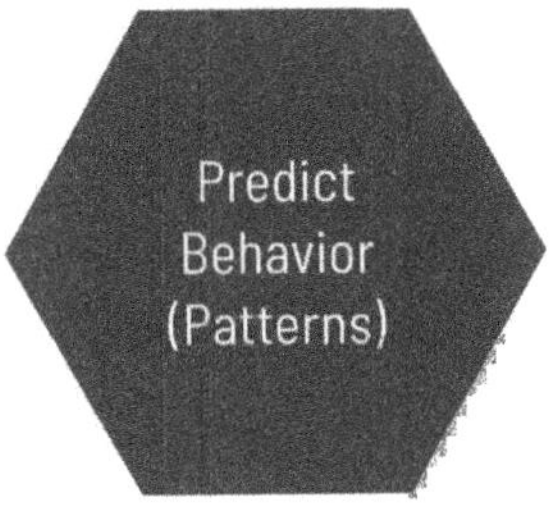

Figure - 4.16

Accessible & Actionable

Data becomes valuable only if it is rich, actionable and accessible. Structured and readily scalable data makes the process of monetisation simpler and efficient, providing higher potential for data monetisation.

Figure - 4.17

Size of the Ecosystem

Businesses with high volume and consequently large data, can generate high value from the data. Companies with national or global scale can easily establish market view, which makes it more meaningful and valuable.

Figure - 4.18

Customer Identification (Granularity)

Data becomes valuable only if it is granular enough to identify the end user. Ability to identify or to profile customers helps in expanding the range of products and services that can be offered.

Figure - 4.19

Figure - 4.20

Uniqueness

Uniqueness of the enterprise data is extremely valuable. It makes the products or services offered by the enterprise exclusive to them and produces a sustainable differentiation, which most organisations yearn for.

Figure - 4.21

Stages to Data Maturity

Based on the maturity of the organisation's data, it can take a call on what kind of a player it wants to be in the market – a data seller or a full-service provider.

Figure - 4.22

Raw Data

Selling raw unprocessed data to outside stakeholders can be a stream for monetisation. Companies with a rich pool of high-quality raw data can sell such data with little investment. Examples are life sciences – related data or even NASDAQ's* Data on Demand service to its ecosystem of partners in the capital markets.

Figure - 4.23

Processed Data

Companies collect and integrate data from multiple sources. Data is processed, stored and leveraged in summary form. Secure capturing and transport of data as well as proper storage and management of data using a data platform can lead to monetisation. For example, card advisory companies provide processed data to merchants and use it for improving its operational efficiency.

Business Intelligence (BI*)/Predictive Insights*

Tools and technologies such as data mining, predictive modelling and analytics convert data into insights. Insights are made available to the stakeholders (both internal and external) to drive business decisions. For example, Walmart* segments its customers into three primary groups, based on purchasing patterns, to spur growth.

Figure - 4.24

Products and Solutions Implementation

This can include data driven interactions with end users. APIs* and ability for companies to access platform and data to build comprehensive products and solutions are also a part of this. Companies use the intelligence to improve products and solutions offering portfolio. For example, Banks use Credit Card customer data to identify customer needs and create new personalised offers.

Figure - 4.25

Security Risks

Software has always been subject to security risks; with AI those risks emerge through the possibility of data manipulation. Three classes of data have an impact on AI systems: input data, training data and test or feedback data.

Figure - 4.26

1. **Input Data**: AI systems feed on input data. They combine this data with a model/ algorithm. to generate an insight. So, just like the old computer adage – 'Garbage In, Garbage Out,' AI fails if it has poor data or bad model. A hacker might cause an AI solution to fail by feeding it with garbage data. E.g. Washington University researchers showed that Google AI could be misled by feeding it with cars' images for fraction of a second so only computers could see but not any human eye. This made the solution to misclassify the videos.

    In an environment where media companies need to do this appropriately to match the correct advertiser, this represents a critical vulnerability.

2. **Training Data Risks** are when someone interrogates your AI solutions/ machines. They may be able to reverse-engineer your algorithms and use your output as their input. E.g. in initial years, Microsoft's Bing was using Internet Explorer's tool bar

to copy Google's search engine. This way, when Google team faked some searches and asked its engineers to use Internet Explorer (IE) for searching those faked keywords for some time, Microsoft picked up those keywords and showed up as results on Bing when somebody from Google team searched those fake terms.

So, issue is that when you have an AI (like Google Search Engine), then if a competitor can observe data being entered (such as a search query) and output being reported (such as a list of websites), then it has the raw materials to employ its own AI to engage in supervised learning and reconstruct the algorithm.

3. **Feedback Data Risk**: AI machines interact with others (human or machine) outside our businesses. Bad actors can feed the AI data that distorts the learning process. This is more than manipulating a single insight, but instead involves teaching the machine to predict incorrectly in a systematic way. E.g. Microsoft launched a twitter chatbot Tay* in March 2016 and let it loose on twitter to interact with people and learn how best to respond. But, soon with bad actors, it became a racist, Nazi sympathizer etc. That is when Microsoft pulled the experiment.

Finding a Starting Point

AI adoption continues to increase, and technology is generating appreciable returns. McKinsey Institute survey shows almost 25% year-on-year increase in the use of AI in standard business processes and across multiple areas of their business. Executives of many companies who have adopted AI, acknowledge that AI has provided rise in business revenues while 40% plus of them also say that AI has reduced costs. It will create $13 trillion of GDP growth by 2030, according to McKinsey, most of which will be in non-internet sectors including manufacturing, agriculture, energy, logistics, and education.

Departments in an Enterprise where AI can be deployed, and savings observed

The rise of AI presents an opportunity for executives in every industry to differentiate their businesses. But implementing a company-wide AI strategy is challenging, especially for legacy* enterprises. It is best to start some small initial projects that can be done in less time (ideally within 6-12 months) and those that have a high chance of success, ideally choosing two/ three projects to increase the chances of creating at least one significant success (Figure 5.1).

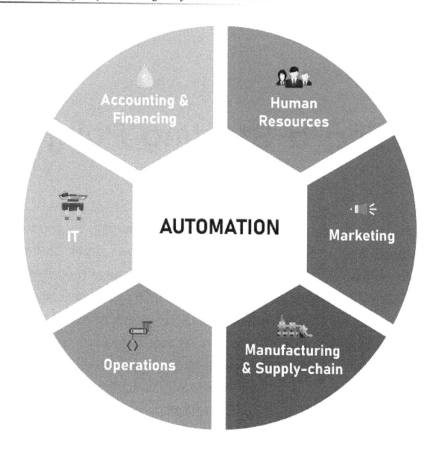

Figure – 5.1

Five Characteristics of a Strong AI Pilot Project

The purpose of starting two to three pilot projects is only partly to create value; more importantly, the success of these first projects will help convince management to invest in building up company's AI capabilities. When considering pilot AI projects, ask yourself the following questions:

1. **Does the project give you a quick win?**

2. **Is the project either too trivial or too unwieldy in size?** For example, will a bot be enough to build, that streamlines customer service or building a face recognition

system be more suitable for instant recognition of customers in the store.

3. **Is your project specific to your industry?** For example, will it be better to make a recruitment bot to scan through candidate resumes at a fast pace in a medical company or is it more valuable to build a health-care-specific AI system— anything ranging from using AI to assist doctors with formulating treatment plans, to streamlining the hospital check-in process through automation, to offering personalized health advice.

4. **Are you accelerating your pilot project with credible partners?** Consider working with external partners to bring in AI expertise quickly. Eventually, you would like to have your own in-house AI team; however, waiting to build a team before executing might be too slow relative to the pace of AI's rise.

5. **Is your project creating value?** Most AI projects create value in one or more of three ways: *reducing costs, increasing revenue* and *diversification* (i.e. launching new lines of business).

Reducing Costs: The two functions, in which the largest cost decrease is reported by companies in individual AI use cases, are manufacturing and supply-chain management. In manufacturing, responses suggest that most significant savings come from optimizing yield and energy. In supply chain management, companies mostly report savings from spend analytics and logistics-network optimization.

Increasing Revenue: Companies report revenue growth in AI use cases in marketing and sales as well as in product and service development. In the former, companies most often report revenue increase from AI use in pricing, prediction of likeliness to buy, and customer-service analytics. In the latter, revenue-producing use cases include the creation of new

AI-based products as well as enhancements. In supply-chain, company executives often cite sales and demand forecasting and spend analytics as use cases that generate revenue.

By sector, the global companies indicated increase in AI/ML adoption in nearly every industry in the year 2018-19 as shown in figure 5.2:

Figure – 5.2

Retail has witnessed the largest increase, with close to 60% global companies saying that they have embedded at least one AI capability in one or more functions or business units. On the other hand, Indian scenario shows that both financial and retail companies are deploying AI on large scale and trying increasingly to deploy AI across domains as shown in figure 5.1. Most logistics and e-commerce companies have deployed robotics to ease out the warehousing and supply chain work or increase efficiency in peak seasons. On the other hand, financial companies are deploying bots* to automate several of their tasks.

Use case examples of Artificial Intelligence

Flavours of Artificial Intelligence in Retail

1. **Conversational commerce – bots*:** chat software/chatbots focussed on helping shoppers make purchases in a conversational text format using natural language processing (NLP*).

2. **Multilingual marketing across multiple channels.**

3. **Predictive merchandising across geographies.**

4. **Real-time product targeting** - machine learning (ML) based real time web page personalisation.

5. **Visual search -** websites let visitors search by image, instead of text, and match relevant products to specific images.

6. **In-store visual monitoring** – to track, stock and promote products in real time.

7. **Real-time pricing & incentives.**

8. **Cashier-less retailing** – sensors and AI enabled shopping carts that enable cashier-less shopping in grocery stores with automatic billing on the mobile devices and payment e-wallets.

9. **Integrated online & in-store analytics** – AI combines both digital & physical store analytics to help retailers better understand their customers.

Figure – 5.3

10. **Multi-channel marketing** - AI creates targeted marketing campaigns across desktop, mobile, email, and other digital channels.

11. **Natural language search** - algorithms that use natural language processing to improve search functionality in e-commerce websites.

12. **Sizing & styling** - AI-powered software will help retailers integrate improved product sizing and outfit-building tools into their websites.

Flavours of Artificial Intelligence in Human Resources

Human Resource department leverages AI technology and solutions in several ways. Figure 5.4 shows some of the following:

> **Talent Discovery:** A wide variety of applications of AI exist in the talent discovery space, often focused on matching talent supply and demand, or predicting recruitment success. Predictors include the job fit (suitability of candidates for jobs), the likelihood that a candidate would be open to exploring a new job opportunity, behavioural profiles through analysis of voice or video interviews, the probability that a candidate would apply for a job, or that the candidate would be hired, etc.

> **Chatbots to support HR service delivery or further process automation**: Automated job assignment, shift scheduling and monitoring, etc.

> **Sentiment Analysis** and theme detection in employee feedback and employee engagement measurement tools.

> **Employee Development** for learning content, mentors, career paths and adaptive learning paths.

> **Job Fit** for checking if the person who applied for a job in some department is fit for that role or merely applying as some of the keywords in his resume match those on the job description of the new position.

> **Employee Skill Matching** refers to a functionality in AI enabled systems which matches skills of all employees in an organisation with all the new jobs coming up and fitment for all people to various such roles. If they are more fit to fulfil the new job roles, they may be given extra duties or replaced with other colleagues of theirs while being shifted to the new role for fulfilment of the duties of the same until new hiring happens.

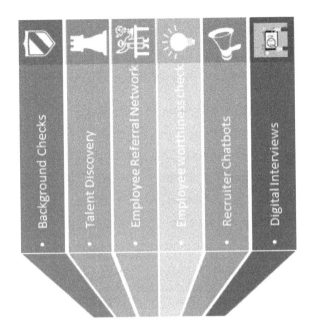

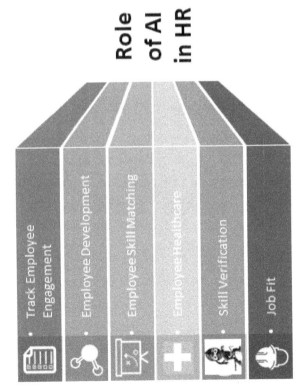

Figure – 5.4

> > **Digital Interviews** are the norm of the day and with increasing digitisation, AI enabled interviewing systems conduct live video interviews while checking prospect's emotion detection, speech analysis, etc. all in real time.

Flavours of Artificial Intelligence in Finance

- **Investment Predictions:** The potential of machine learning technology to disrupt the investment banking industry is being taken seriously by major institutions. JP Morgan, Bank of America, and Morgan Stanley are developing automated investment advisors, powered by machine learning technology. Wise fintech* companies, likewise, are likely to follow suit.

- **Algorithmic Trading:** Algorithmic systems are often making millions of trades in a day, hence the term 'high-frequency trading' (HFT), which is a subset of algorithmic trading. Most hedge funds and financial institutions do not openly disclose their AI approaches to trading (for good reason), but it is believed that machine learning and deep learning are playing an increasingly important role in calibrating trading decisions in real time.

- **Loan/Insurance Underwriting:** Underwriting could be described as a perfect job for machine learning in finance, and indeed there is a great deal of worry in the industry that machines will replace a large swath of the underwriting positions that exist today.

- **Security-2.0**: Usernames, passwords, and security questions may no longer be the norm for user security in next five years. User security in banking and finance is a particularly high stakes game (one would probably share one's Facebook* login to the world than release one's bank account information to a small group of strangers, and for good reason). In addition to anomaly-detection applications like those currently being developed and used in fraud, future security measures might require facial recognition, voice recognition, or other biometric data.

- AI & ML are used for **risk management** through early and more accurate estimation of risks. Artificial intelligence and machine learning are used for anticipating and detecting fraud, suspicious transactions, defaulters, and the risk of cyber-attacks, resulting in better risk management.

Artificial Intelligence use cases currently existing in Sales:

The number of applications for AI in sales is growing daily. McKinsey & Company predicts AI will contribute $1.4 to $2.6 trillion of value in marketing and sales. Here are just a few examples of what AI is doing for sales:

- Analyse which leads are most likely to convert into deals.

- Analyse past deals and discover how to use that information to structure new deals.

- Analyse sales pipeline and create a highly accurate sales forecast (better than 90 percent).

- Provide sales reps AI-generated response suggestions during live customer conversations.

- Analyse the next best action for salespeople to follow, after a customer conversation.

(Ref: https://www.sellingpower.com)

Artificial Intelligence use cases currently existing in Social domains

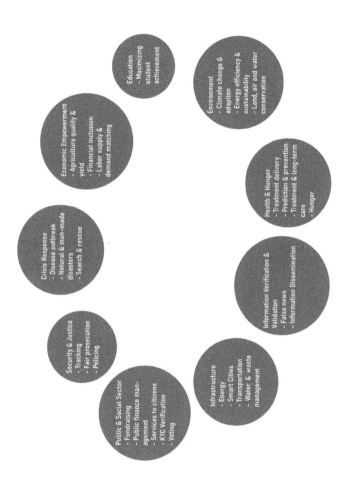

ARTIFICIAL INTELLIGENCE USE CASES CURRENTLY EXISTING IN SOCIAL DOMAINS

Figure – 5.5

(Source: McKinsey Global Institute Analysis, Wikipedia)

What are the Areas most susceptible to Automation?

Companies which have either not adopted Artificial Intelligence yet or are afraid of doing so or exploring adopting the technology, all have same question in mind i.e.

What all tasks are there that can be automated with Artificial Intelligence?

Figure 5.6 shows the tasks that can be automated with artificial intelligence:

As per the figure below - **Managing Others,** being a human resource management task, is the least susceptible task that can be automated as robots or machines lack emotions, empathy, sympathy etc. - attributes that are indispensable in human interactions and play a vital role for positive outcomes.

Applying expertise is also least susceptible to automation by artificial intelligence as this also involves decision making on human part. Decision making, though has started seeing automation in some countries and in some very large organisations where a board seat has been given to AI, yet still does not involve applying expertise physically or in real sense.

Customer Interactions have started getting automated with artificial intelligence through bots and virtual agents. But they too are mostly over online systems. Physical robots with customer interactivity are very limited as of today but increasingly being worked upon to make them more intelligent.

Unpredictable physical work is slowly getting automated through robotics like in warehousing and healthcare domain.

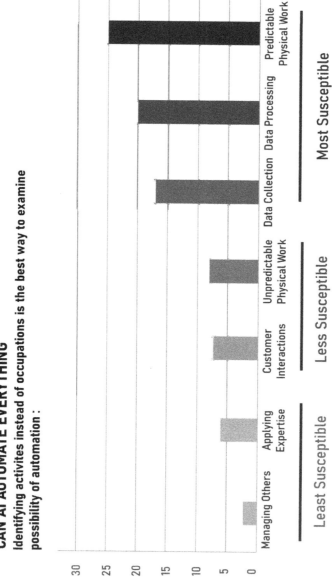

Figure – 5.6

(Source.: McKinsey, USA)

Data Collection, Data Processing and Predictable Physical Work are the most susceptible tasks to get automated by artificial intelligence.

What are artificial intelligence use cases currently existing in companies?

Figure 5.7 shows the current use cases of AI by percentage of resources spent in companies globally:

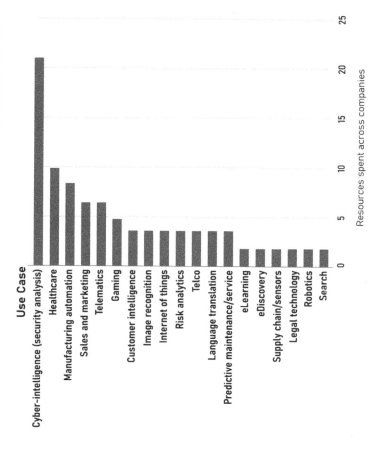

Figure – 5.7

(Source.: O'Reilly)

Setting up your AI Project for Success

AI is automation on steroids. A rich source of ideas for AI projects will lie in automating tasks that humans are doing today. You will find that ***AI is good at automating tasks, rather than jobs***. Try to identify the specific tasks that people are doing and examine if any of them can be automated. For executing an AI pilot project, it is recommended to clearly state the desired timeline and outcome, and allocate a reasonable budget to the team and to pursue following steps:

i) **Appoint a leader:** Choose someone who can work cross-functionally and bridge both AI & your industry's domain experts. This will ensure that when the project succeeds, it will influence the rest of the organization. The leader's goal is not to build an AI start-up rather his goal is to build a successful project that will influence management's beliefs and state of knowledge about AI, as a first step towards building future projects.

ii) **Conduct business value and technical diligence:** It is advisable to pick up a project that is feasible. Also ensure that, if executed successfully, project will create sufficient value for the business. Technical diligence can take a few weeks, requiring a technical team to examine what data you have and perhaps even carry out small-scale experiments.

iii) **Build a small team:** Numerous pilot ideas are executed with about 5 to 15 people. The exact level of resources may vary widely per project, but scoping projects, that can be done with a small team, ensures that everyone knows everyone else and work cross-functionally, and perhaps also make the allocation of resources less painful.

iv) **Communicate:** When the pilot project hits key milestones, and delivers successful result, ensure to give the team an internal platform—ranging from talks, to awards, to even external PR—to allow their work to become known inside the company. Making sure the project team is recognized by the CEO and is visibly successful, will be a key part to building momentum. If you have an AI technology team working with a business team, make sure also that the business team receives plenty of credit and rewards for the success. This will encourage other business teams to jump into AI as well.

Most Efficient Ways for AI Enablement

When we have taken care of various aspects like skills/ talent required, data types and formats, the starting point identification etc., the buck stops at 'what strategy to adopt for AI enablement of an enterprise?' This chapter discusses various approaches an enterprise can take for AI enablement as well as suggests the most efficient ways which various enterprises adopt based on their management decisions and/ or preferences.

AI Enablement of an Enterprise involves Five steps

1. Core AI Resource Assimilation using Funding or Acquisition.

2. Gain Senior Management support.

3. Focus on Process not Function.

4. Reskill your teams and HR-Redeployment.

5. Encourage Innovation.

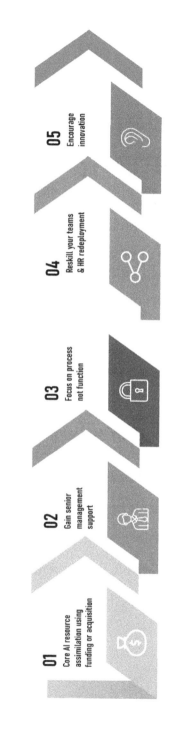

Figure – 6.1

(Source: AI & Analytics, Wiley)

1. Core AI Resource Assimilation using Funding or Acquisition:

Some of the AI resources are those discussed in previous chapters like data, skills/ talent required and starting point identification. Other AI resources are data formats, hardware and cloud-infrastructure*, etc. In absence of talent or skills, acquisition of other smaller AI focussed companies can be done so that talent problem can be solved at one go. Doing this, will enable bringing at least one AI product into enterprise's portfolio without waiting to make it. Even if it's an AI services company which is being acquired, expertise comes in that helps in transformation of different departments inside the enterprise in faster mode.

2. Gaining Senior Management Support:

Maximum resistance is faced from C-Suite*. Regulatory uncertainty about Artificial Intelligence, rough experiences with previous technology innovations and a defensive posture to better protect shareholders – not stakeholders – are some contributing factors. Lack of understanding of technology benefits can adversely affect the bottom lines and even cause the enterprises to go out of business. Pursuing AI without senior management involvement is difficult so getting their wholehearted support is an absolute must.

3. Focusing on the Process and not on the Function:

Critical element that differentiates AI Success from AI Failure is *Strategy*. ***AI cannot be deployed in piecemeal fashion. It must be part of the enterprises' overall business plan along with aligned resources, structures, and processes***.

This includes the following (Figure 6.3):

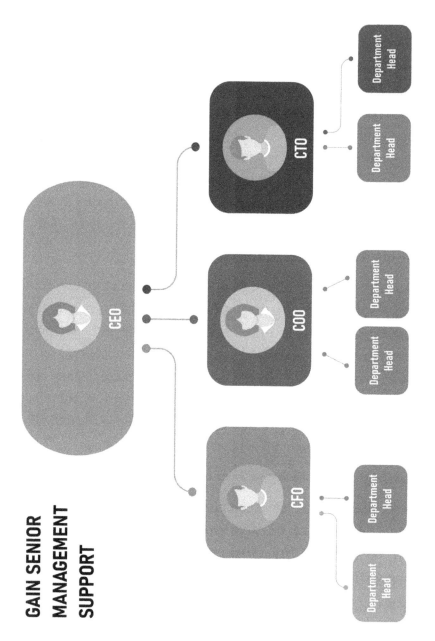

Figure – 6.2

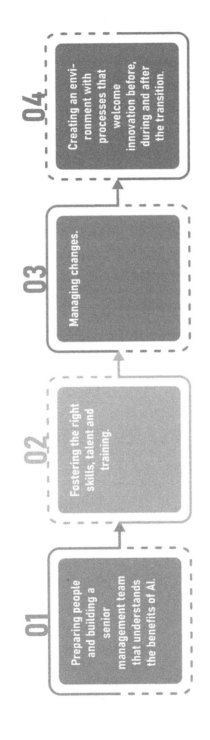

PROCESS-BASED FOCUS RATHER THAN FUNCTION-BASED

01 Preparing people and building a senior management team that understands the benefits of AI.

02 Fostering the right skills, talent and training.

03 Managing changes.

04 Creating an environment with processes that welcome innovation before, during and after the transition.

Figure – 6.3

(Source: AI & Analytics, Wiley)

4. **Reskilling your team and HR Re-deployment:**

HR department heads and corporate management will need to figure out new jobs for employees to do. Redeployment is a crucial factor that agile* companies learn to handle. The question of job losses is a sensitive issue that often pops up in headlines. But Artificial Intelligence also creates numerous job opportunities in new and different areas, often encouraging employees to learn higher skills.

Given the enormous potential of AI to complement human intelligence, it is vital for top executives to appraise reskilling possibilities. It is in the best interest for them to train and re-train employees (who are being moved from jobs that are getting automated by AI) to jobs where there is still potential.

5. **Encouraging Innovations:**

ENCOURAGING INNOVATIONS

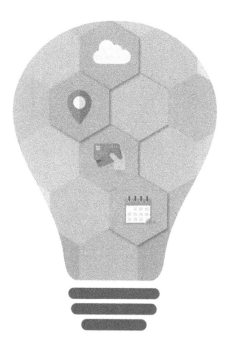

Figure – 6.4

Organization's culture plays a big role in transformation processes. Merely, putting posters around does not bring innovations. For this, top management and thence HR must train managers to have more patience and let employees experiment and innovate. Employees should be given some leeway on extent of mistakes tolerated and not reprimanded for. The way it works is to identify and drive visible examples of adoption. Example, algorithmic trading, image recognition, tagging and patient data processing are predicted to top the AI use cases by 2025. As per Tractica*, predictive maintenance* and content distribution* on social media are slated to be the 4th and 5th highest revenue producing AI use cases over next 5 years.

Build, Buy or Outsource AI Deployment

We have discussed above, various aspects involved in AI enablement of an enterprise. But, while 'identifying AI use cases' may be challenging, 'actual implementation' is a whole lot more complex. Thus, while these discussions start, the top management faces this dilemma all the time - **Whether to build, buy or outsource the deployment of AI?**

Figure 6.5 shows eight questions that should be discussed internally (i.e. within an enterprise) about *which solution path is best suited to one's enterprise:*

8 QUESTIONS ABOUT "WHICH SOLUTION PATH IS BEST SUITED FOR AI DEPLOYMENT"

Has enterprise access to AI/ML talent?

Does enterprise's domain require it to be agile?

Is industry such that new kinds of data have become available or a new business has become amenable to analytics?

Is enterprise's analytics scenario unique?

Is analytics a critical differentiator for the business?

Is there a bundled application available that meets criteria/requirements but is difficult to implemement because tech-stack is too exotic or idiosyncratic?

Is there a bundled application availability that meets enterprise's requirements?

Is there a package application available that exactly solves the analytical problem at hand?

Figure – 6.5

1. **Is there a packaged application available that exactly solves the analytical problem at hand?**

Using a packaged app is typically the fastest route to applying machine learning and analytics. According to a Gartner research, analytics applications and performance management represent 15% of the total spends in the entire Business Intelligence (BI*) and Analytics market. Use your resources in exploring your current vendor relationships to evaluate their offerings, especially the packaged solutions.

2. **Is there a bundled application available that meets many, though not all, of enterprise's requirements?**

Even if there is no perfectly suited application that meets hundred percent of the problem at hand, there are times when one can get a good enough solution that delivers rapid return-on-investment. Time required to get a solution and advantage of packaged applications, can minimise opportunity costs. Such apps can also serve as a stopgap measure (measure which is taken for the time being) until other ideal solutions become available and implemented.

3. **Is there a bundled application available that meets the criteria of the requirements, but is difficult to implement because technology stack is too complex to use?**

Bundled app vendors or a third party may be able to customise a packaged app to suit the challenging requirements of tech-stack. This will cut into time to solution and cost savings, but the customised app may still be one's best option. Enabling new analytics initiatives may also be the motivation an enterprise needs to consider converting to a more conventional stack and/ or updating its aging technologies.

4. **Is analytics a critical differentiator for your business?**

The scale or distinctiveness of your business could enable greater potential benefits from best-in-class analytics than what your competitors can achieve. If so, building or outsourcing your analytics solution is likely the best approach. Buying bundled apps is a good option only when addressing common and relatively straightforward business problems. Businesses that achieve best-in-class ML and analytics solutions and that disrupt their industries typically do so through a build strategy or an outsource strategy.

While best-in-class analytics is a tempting and often worthwhile proposition, the potential difficulty of attaining such a solution and the risk of project failure means you should also reconsider bundled application (point 2 above).

5. Is your analytics scenario unique?

If you feel your analytics solution is truly unique, you must consider building it 'in-house' as in these cases new and custom analytics solutions require a great deal of business understanding. Stakeholders need to understand – 1. why a problem needs to be solved, – 2. how the solution will gel with the analytics status quo and – 3. what the future implications of the applied solution will be for business. Packaged/ bundled solutions providers will not be able to comprehend your problem at hand so well.

6. Is your industry such that new kinds of data have become available or a new business has become amenable to analytics?

This is a rare situation with enormous upside for organisations with the right analytics mindset. If new kinds of data have become available to you, reconsider building it in-house (point 5 above). In novel analytics situations, it is highly likely that no applicable packaged application is available yet, as vendors and service providers may not have had time to acquire experience in handling this new data or process. It will be wise of you to weigh the cost and benefits of obtaining first mover advantage within your industry (examples of successes include Amazon's* recommendation engine*, NIKI* and Yellow-messenger* bots also being widely accepted services and many more).

7. Does your domain require you to be agile*?

Agility* is highly prized within domains that are subject to rapid changes all the time like financial markets, social media or the convergence of operations technology with information technology. Here analytics platforms offer the highest levels of agility and granularity of control. The built operations enable the most rapid change as analytics teams can tweak and redeploy models to reflect changing business conditions. The ability to create adaptive models that learn and recalibrate themselves is also available with some analytics platforms.

8. Do you have access to AI/ML talent?

If you do not have data scientists on your team, consider bringing in some at the earliest to bring them up – to speed of your business. If your staff lacks analytics skills, de-emphasize generic-analytics platforms and crowdsourcing or talent marketplaces, as both require firm grasp of analytics and data science skills and score the lowest for ease of use. Even if your long-term plan is the build option, consider outsourcing part of your entire pilot project to get your analytics initiative off the ground. This partly will help introduce best practices to one's organisation early, on your AI journey and protect you from common pitfalls (such as scope-creep or poor data quality).

Clearly, there are advantages and disadvantages in all the three options (i.e. build, buy or outsource AI deployment). So, each one of these is discussed here for clear understanding.

Let's start with **Buy** option first as it looks like the easiest option.

Buy Artificial Intelligence from Third Parties

This is the easiest option if one has funds. When talking about AI, most people think of the latest consumer applications such as interacting with Amazon Echo* or Google Duplex* automating smart homes. Partly due to these well-known applications, you would naturally consider Amazon* or Google* as potential partners when planning your own AI activities. There are several good reasons to buy AI as a service from large AI service providers like Googles and Amazons of the world.

Building AI solutions require four ingredients (shown in figure 6.6), which can be provided by third-party AI service providers:

4 INGREDIENTS FOR BUILDING ARTIFICIAL INTELLIGENCE SOLUTIONS

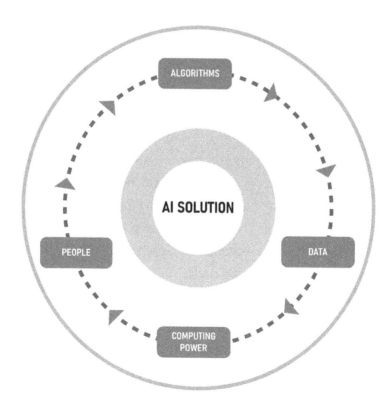

Figure – 6.6

1. **Algorithms***: Most sophisticated algorithms are available for free nowadays on sites like GitHub, Kaggle etc. and most academics as well as coders make their algorithms open to share their models in such repositories along with the code so algorithms don't play a major role in the build or buy decision process.

2. **Data**: Large data sets are a prerequisite for AI solutions to be developed along with quality and amount of data. These three determine the accuracy and, thus, the commercial benefit of the respective AI models. In some cases, AI service providers manage to pool own and third-party data to a breadth and depth, difficult to match for any individual enterprise.

3. **Computing power:** One can simply leverage the global infrastructure of AI service providers (Amazon Web Services, Microsoft and Google – all the three being the biggest - besides many other smaller players). It is economical in comparison to pre-cloud era - super computers, highly flexible, and have reliable, scalable, and globally available computing power instead of building these capabilities in-house.

4. **People:** Despite recent growth, the academic community working on machine learning — the powerhouse of modern AI — has been quite small and getting weaned out as big giants are attracting them at fat pay packages from universities. Consequently, only a few seasoned professionals work in the field. The resulting AI talent war has been fought with exuberant salary offers and has led to a concentration of AI expertise in a few companies/ developed cities across the world and in companies such as Google, Apple, Amazon etc. Due to this concentration of talent as well as the difficulty and costs of assembling a top-notch AI team, we may find ourselves better off collaborating with large service providers.

Above reasoning can conclude our decision towards – Buy

AI service providers can provide us with a cost-efficient and globally scalable infrastructure, offer more accurate models due to their access to more data and are able to provide us with cutting edge AI expertise as they have hired many of the brightest minds in AI. So why should we even bother building our own proprietary AI solutions?

Outsource AI Deployment

While buy is a good option, outsourcing is probably equally good or more popular option and is mostly adopted by companies due to lack of internal team, motivation etc. However, in many cases, even this is not an option due to two reasons primarily. First is **Customer Data Sensitivity*** and second, the **Competitive Advantage based on their own exclusive datasets.** The value of AI models mainly lies within the data used to train, test and calibrate the model, so sharing this source of value with third parties should be avoided.

Build Inhouse AI Enablement Capability

This is by far the best way for AI enablement of an enterprise and can be done in two ways again i.e. **Build Own Capability** or **Build Internal AI Experimentation & Training Lab**:

Build Own Capability: Most companies, who try building their own capability, do this by hiring new talents equipped with these skills in spurts and rely on online-learning platforms, universities, and executive-level programs to train existing employees. Trainers are hired for low level workers for skill development. But this results in a short- term venture as outsourced trainers are just that, they visit the company, train the people and go away without worrying about if what they trained people on, is being used effectively on deployments, etc. Thus, it costs the company dearly as lot of time, money and energy is wasted without any fruitful results. This results in company losing trust in the viability and use of AI in their processes. Rarely does it happen in a company where some internal heads are able to make some good use of the talent developed.

Build Internal AI Experimentation & Training Lab

There is no 'one-template-fit-all' approach, but the rise of AI is one of the defining business opportunities for leaders today. Associated with it is the challenge of creating an organization that can rise to that opportunity and exploit the potential of AI at scale.

In the 5-step enterprise AI building process (as discussed at the beginning of this chapter), it is shown that getting top management indulgence is an absolute must for effective AI deployment. Thus, meeting this challenge requires enterprises to prepare their leaders, business staff, analytics teams, and end users to work and think in new ways. It not only helps them to understand how to tap AI effectively, but also teaches them to embrace data exploration, agile* development, and interdisciplinary teamwork. Focus should be on to develop broad capability building across all levels.

The answer to the talent challenge, in the author's experience, is to create an in-house analytics academy. These unique analytics-training centres are relatively a new development. The author believes in wholistic training and upskilling can only happen when all seniors and juniors sit together, collaborate, co-create, and co-learn. Further, if one has to learn to scale and operate at high levels, one must teach because that's when we put in more labour to understand things at the core and are able to answer any challenges that we face in our professional lives.

This topic of building Internal AI Experimentation & Training Lab demands to be discussed as a separate chapter altogether in the book to get justified attention. Hence, readers are advised to refer the next (i.e. 7th.) chapter titled 'The Rise of the Internal AI Labs' for detailed discussion. It explains what an internal experimentation and training AI Lab can do that other approaches fail to accomplish.

The Rise of the Internal AI Labs

The author's experience in training and consulting suggests that internal AI Lab can play a crucial role in developing an AI-focussed and contextually AI-educated workforce in a concerted manner, providing an effective way to fulfil many essential requirements for successful AI efforts, as below:

- **A common vision, language, and protocol** across trainings ensure that all stakeholders (i.e. executives, business teams, analytics teams, and frontline staff) align around the core elements necessary to embed AI into their business successfully, to apply the same methods when identifying and developing solutions, and to understand each other's roles and responsibilities. Doing so, makes the knowledge gained similar across the organisation.

  Knowledge and learned experiences from previous AI use cases, ensure support from leaders, and promote community building so that teams run like well-oiled machines, capable of building a minimum viable product much more quickly.

  It also enables organizations to deploy talent where it is needed, which not only maximizes expertise across the business but also boosts retention of highly sought-after experts, such as data scientists, whose job-satisfaction is often closely intertwined with opportunities to learn and grow by working on a variety of different business problems.

- **Customized content linked to company's goals, starting point, and industry context** ensures that training translates into business value. To this end, AI Lab team designs learning programs that consider their client companies' transformation road map, as well as their 'cultural barriers' and 'skill gaps' that could derail the progress.

Companies tailor learning-journeys to their business and workforce needs, articulating how skills will enable the desired outcomes. For example, AI Lab, ensures leaders are well-versed in AI so they can develop and execute a strategy that pushes them ahead of the competition. They (the companies) are equipped to offer their business staff, the technical knowledge to translate business needs into AI solutions. They enable data scientists, data engineers, and other technical experts not only to stay on top of rapid innovations in their field but also to learn how to collaborate with their business colleagues effectively so that they focus on the business problems that will derive the greatest value.

- **Active apprenticeships help bring classroom theory to life**, enabling participants to learn by doing, and facilitate employee growth from a 'learner' (who has a classroom understanding of a topic) to a 'practitioner' (who is skilled at capability delivery) and, ultimately, to an 'expert' (who can lead in their function). In some cases, such as building translator expertise, this fieldwork is especially critical. Just like medical school graduates need residency training to build their diagnostics, translators benefit from similar guidance as they learn.

Building an effective AI Lab internally varies across companies but some critical components have come to light while studying the viability of these AI Labs (Figure 7.1):

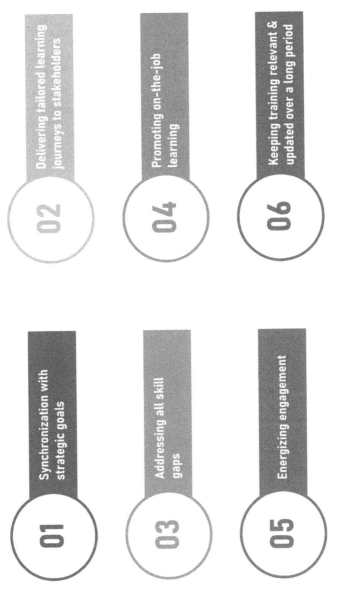

CRITICAL COMPONENTS FOR STUDYING VIABILITY
OF AI LABS IN COMPANIES

01 — Synchronization with strategic goals

02 — Delivering tailored learning journeys to stakeholders

03 — Addressing all skill gaps

04 — Promoting on-the-job learning

05 — Energizing engagement

06 — Keeping training relevant & updated over a long period

Figure – 7.1

Important steps to building the Internal AI LAB

1. **Tie Training to transformation:** AI Lab training is most effective when it is aligned with company's AI-Roadmap. By knowing how newly acquired skills will further the company's goals, they can ensure the right kind of training for various levels of people from top echelons to bottom.

2. **Leave No role behind:** As mentioned above, 'various kinds of training for various kinds of roles in an organisation right from top management to middle managers to bottom developers and also to story tellers as and when need arises', will lead to effective training of all roles involved in the companies.

3. **Go beyond Mathematics:** Whenever employees come to know of AI initiatives, they are generally apprehensive about being asked to brush up their Maths skills but successful company's internal AI Labs go beyond and provide grounded foundational courses to upskill the employees as well as take into consideration and emphasize organisational and cultural changes critical for big organisations to succeed in today's fiercely competitive world.

4. **Blend 'book smarts' with 'street smarts':** Successful labs also combine classroom theory and real work so participants learn by doing and can advance the company's agenda at the same time.

5. **Energize engagement:** Successful labs position training for prime roles, such as data scientists, as a privilege. For example, business leaders nominate high performers for Analyst/ translator training, who are then approved by the company's chair, vice chair, head of analytics, and lab training program head. Likewise, data-science and data-engineering candidates must be cleared for training following a technical-assessment test. Then company celebrates achievements, including individual completion of courses, team

completion of projects and delivery of value, and overall attainment of organizational milestones, such as completion of priority use cases. High performers are awarded trophies at the annual company meeting in front of an impressive strength of leaders.

6. **Keep it relevant:** AI technologies are constantly evolving, and technical experts need to stay up to date on AI techniques, tools, and supporting technologies. Talent comes and goes, and new hires need to acquire organisational knowledge quickly. As changes happen, cross-functional teams find better ways of working together, which must finally, be pushed back into the ecosystem. For this, they do the following:

   - **Cultivate Internal Faculty**: While organizations typically launch their Centre of Excellence (CoE*) using external faculty, author's endeavour remains to train the CoE stakeholders and others inside the organisations to co-facilitate programs during the second and third waves of training. Over time, they are given increasing ownership for leading classes. By the fourth wave of training, they transition from teaching assistants to lead instructors, receiving behind-the-scenes coaching as needed from higher management or outside stake trainers from appropriate sources.

   - **Creating an Internal Leadership Team:** Responsible for growing the internal AI Lab, this leadership team continually updates the curriculum to bring real-world experience back into the classrooms. This team within its Centre of Excellence, reports directly to the head of analytics, to oversee AI Lab growth. This team will likely include an AI Lab dean and content managers for each learning track, along with support from the company's learning planners in HR.

Driving capacity and capability building internally has been proven at large organisations like Google, Amazon, and Ubers of the world as the best form of AI capability development seen anywhere in the world till date. Diverse workforce requires the targeted learning journeys that AI labs are expressly designed to deliver. And as the technology continues to evolve, so too will labs, to ensure workers are equipped for whatever lies ahead.

Precautions to take while doing AI Deployment to Avoid Misfire

In the previous chapters, the author has covered basics to advanced topics on what it will take to deploy AI in any enterprise. However, there are certain precautions the management should take for effective long-term implementation with least of hiccups in deployment or in maintaining the status quo.

Figure 8.1 illustrates certain potential pitfalls to avoid when introducing AI in an enterprise.

Incomplete Knowledge: One must avoid different knowledge bases from across service channels to prevent giving customers – conflicting information. This happens, for example, when data bases are incomplete and provide customer's information in bits and pieces, misleading the customer to understand something else. This is frequently seen in disconnected systems in small/ medium healthcare providing facilities, etc.

One Size Fits All Strategy: This strategy is not advisable as all businesses and problems demand their own set of configuration, algorithms, and data bases.

POTENTIAL PITFALLS TO AVOID WHEN INTRODUCING AI

Incomplete Knowledge	One-size-fits-all strategy	Lack of access to customer data	Insufficient training of AI systems	Absence of performance metrics
Using different knowledge databases from across different service channels, giving conflicting informations to customers	One size fits all strategy is not sound, as differing types of businesses and problems demand their own set of configurations	Virtual agents and AI systems dont have the same access to customer data while rolling out an AI enhanced customer service department	Failing to continuosly train and update AI systems	In this situation, required parameters, data, models, etc. require continuous tweaking

Figure – 8.1

Lack of Access to Customer Data: When rolling out an AI-enhanced customer service department, ensure that the virtual agents/ AI systems have the same access to customer data as the live agents have.

Insufficient Training of AI Systems: Humans require continuous training on updated business insights and trends, likewise artificial intelligence systems too require continuous training on new data generated, as with the passage of time business grows/ declines, requirements change or policies shift.

Absence of Performance Metrics: Every bit of data going into a machine counts and thus presence of performance metrics is also required to be judged to ascertain if things are going in the right direction. If not, the required parameters, data, models or anything else – require continuous tweaking until desired performance is met.

From the above points, it becomes obvious that data plays an important role and cannot be compromised. Data is most crucial part of the AI domain. If not whole, at least 90% of the problems can be avoided if data is adequate, right kind of data is there and following precautionary measures are taken to avoid common errors:

9 COMMON ERRORS TO BE AVOIDED

COVERAGE ERROR (E.g. survey of only iOS users instead of Android as well on smartphone usage)

INFERENCE ERROR (are made by statistical or machine learning models when they make incorrect predictions from the available ground truth)

UNKOWN ERROR (data about what a user did on any site can be collected but not his motive behind his action leading to errors)

MEASUREMENT ERROR (when the h/w or s/w used to capture data goes awry, e.g. headphones/speaker phone recording)

SAMPLING ERROR (smaller sample size instead of target sample size)

PROCESSING ERROR (For e.g. due to very old data or a new team etc.)

UNDEFINED GOALS (of collection hence, bad/wrong data collection happens)

DATA DEFINITION ERROR (numerous assumptions would need to be mentioned like, calendar vs. fiscal year)

CAPTURE ERROR (incorrect mechanism can lead to capturing incorrect or accidentally biased data)

Figure – 8.2

(Source: Topbots)

1. **Undefined Goals** - If the problem is not defined correctly, data collectors end up collecting wrong data which can lead to fallacious results later.

2. **Measurement Error** - When the hardware or software used to collect the data is of poor quality or goes awry. E.g., using a mobile camera (instead of high definition camera) to take pictures, leading to images of low resolution.

3. **Coverage Error** - Considering only web users and leaving mobile web users.

4. **Data Definition Error** – E.g., taking a fiscal calendar into consideration instead of the financial calendar. In such a case, many assumptions will need to be mentioned, etc.

5. **Sample Size** - Sample size is skewed instead of taking actual sample size desired for effective training of the algorithm.

6. **Inference Error** - This occurs when wrong kind of statistical or machine learning models are used to generate insights.

7. **Capture Error** - Incorrect mechanisms can lead to capturing incorrect or accidentally biased data.

8. **Processing Error** - This happens when old or new team is assigned data handling aspects.

9. **Unknown Error:** Data is generally collected by site owners on what a user did on any site, but data on his motives behind his actions, is not collected which can lead to incompleteness in the data and later on when this data is put through the algorithms and machines, errors in the insights are generated.

Overfitting & Underfitting

'Overfitting' is the production of an analysis that corresponds too closely or exactly to a set of data and may, therefore, fail to fit additional data or to predict future observations reliably.

'Underfitting', on the other hand, occurs when a statistical model cannot adequately capture the underlying structure of the data.

Example: An autonomous car trained in USA will be said to be overfitted to US road conditions and underfitted to Indian road conditions. Another example could be - customer data features used for marketing for a small company may be over fitted to small company and underfitted for large company as many more features would be required from customer data for marketing appropriately for the large company.

Bias*

Bias and unfairness are complex human notions. While 'bias' can refer to any form of preference, 'unfair' means unwanted or undesirable bias—that is, discrimination against certain individuals or groups of individuals based on the inappropriate use of certain traits. Perhaps the most discussed forms of "unfair bias" relate to attributes or groups such as disabilities, race and gender. This along with others is certainly an exhaustive list.

Data is often the source of bias

While bias has always been considered as "algorithmic bias," the underlying data, rather than the algorithm itself, is most often the main source of the issue. Here, some researchers make a useful distinction and separate the model into two different algorithms—**the trainer**, which can be biased by the underlying data and the training process, and **the screener**, which simply makes predictions based on the trainer.

Models may be trained on data containing human decisions or on data that reflect second-order effects of societal or historical inequities. For example, word embeddings (a set of natural language processing techniques) trained on news articles may exhibit the gender stereotypes found in the society.

Such biases are often encoded by other variables even when algorithms are prevented from considering protected characteristics directly. For example, in the hiring algorithm, the system learns to favour words that are more commonly found on male's applications, such as "executed" or "captured."

Bias can also be introduced into the data through how they are collected or selected for use. In criminal justice models, oversampling certain neighbourhoods because they are overpoliced can result in more recorded crime, which results in more policing. In financial decision making, under sampling certain groups could lead to models that approve groups of applicants at lower rates.

Data generated by users can also create a feedback loop that leads to bias. Given the number of algorithms reacting to billions of user actions every day, this is an increasingly important potential source of bias.

Finally, a machine learning algorithm may pick up on statistical correlations that are societally unacceptable or illegal. For example, if a mortgage lending model finds that older individuals have a higher likelihood of defaulting and reduces lending based on age, society and legal institutions may consider this to be illegal age discrimination.

The 'absence of unwanted bias' is not enough to conclude that a system is 'fair'. To the extent AI is used for decision making, prediction, and allocative efficiency, it will always be subject to challenges of bias and fairness. But our endeavour should always be to be as unbiased as possible in our data collection, algorithm development etc., else it will hinder the decisions taken in the enterprise at some point in time.

Ethics* in AI

Tech giants such as Alphabet*, Amazon*, Facebook*, IBM* and Microsoft* – as well as individuals like Stephen Hawking* and Elon

Musk* – believe that now is the right time to talk about the nearly boundless landscape of artificial intelligence. In many ways, this is just as much a new frontier for ethics and risk assessment as it is for emerging technology.

Following are some of the main issues that keep AI experts up at night?

1. Unemployment. What happens after the end of jobs?

The hierarchy of labour is concerned primarily with automation. As we've invented ways to automate jobs, we could create room for people to assume more complex roles, moving from the physical work that dominated the pre-industrial era to the cognitive labour that characterizes strategic and administrative work in our globalized society.

Let us consider trucking - it currently employs millions of individuals in the United States alone. What would happen to them if the self-driving trucks promised by Tesla's Elon Musk become widely available in the next decade? But on the other hand, if we consider the lower risk of accidents, self-driving trucks seem like an ethical as well as a rational choice. The same scenario could happen to office workers, as well as to most of the workforce in developed countries.

2. Inequality.

Graph (figure 5.6) in the fifth chapter already shows that lesser skilled tasks are automatable. But this automation is already taking up huge number of low skilled jobs thus giving rise to unemployment and thus inequality between the rich (who can get trained in higher skills by paying hefty fee of the universities) and the not so skilled poor/low wage employees.

3. Humanity.

Many scientists world-over are pondering about negative impact AI is going to have on the humanity. Most AI tools are and will be in the hands of companies striving for profits or governments striving for power. Values and ethics are often not inculcated into the digital systems. These systems are globally networked and not easy to regulate or rein in.

The efficiencies and other economic advantages of code-based machine intelligence will continue to disrupt all aspects of human work. While some expect new jobs will emerge, others worry about massive job losses, widening economic divides and social upheavals, including populist uprisings.

4. Racist robots.

As the saying goes 'Garbage-In, Garbage-Out', in similar fashion, the computer systems and AI systems are also dependent on what we feed them with. Our biases and prejudices in our data also feed them with same biases and prejudices, thus making them racist. There have been instances world-over where AI systems/ bots used in recruitments have shown bias towards men or whites trashing the resumes belonging to women and blacks. Fear is lurking across the world that in future, we may have to live our lives on the mercy of some ill-trained biased robots.

5. Security.

There have been talks by leaders across the globe where likes of Elon Musk and others have said things like – in future, high-end air force jets will become obsolete as AI enabled high-end drones will replace these jets and thus costly/trained fighters' pilots will not be required any longer. If this becomes a reality, power will be held by only a relatively small number of countries capable of putting in huge monies in such systems while leaving other countries vulnerable to automated attacks by such forces. Many engineers of Google revolted saying they will not work on advance AI warfare systems being developed by likes of US Armed Forces and others and many scientists and large company leaders welcomed this action and ethical preference of these engineers.

6.   Robot Rights*

Some ethical questions exist about mitigating suffering, some about risking negative outcomes. While we consider these risks, we should also keep in mind that, overall, this technological progress means better lives for everyone. Artificial intelligence has vast potential, and its responsible implementation is up to us.

Most of the above risks can and should be taken care of and can be achieved by creating a powerful data-oriented culture in the enterprise to bring together data, talent, tools and decision making so that data becomes the default support for company operations. It can be done by following some or all the following ways:

1.   C-suite team includes at least one data leader.

2.   Data are broadly accessible to frontline employees whenever needed: To do this well, often requires reconfiguring organizational processes to allow the rapid sharing of data, for example, by setting up a data marketplace; building technical infrastructure; making use of automation to identify, catalogue, and manage data at scale; and employing common querying and visualization tools across the enterprise to support widespread data use; they should treat data as an internal product to be packaged and distributed to groups across the enterprise, and manage it as such.

3. Culture supports rapid testing and iterations based on data and tolerates fast failure i.e. 'Fail Early-Fail Fast' approach.

4. Hiring criteria for non-management roles include proficiency in data-related topics.

5. Hiring criteria for management roles include proficiency in data-related topics.

6. Company-wide education on data topics.

7. Attracting and retaining the best talent is a pressing need among high performing organisations and increasingly other companies too.

8. Maintaining modern robust data architecture to support the rapid collection and sharing of data that enables frontline employees to access and utilize the data they need.

AI's Future Trends & Potential

Progress in AI is an interesting paradox; on the one hand, there is an advancement on the research side in machine learning and deep learning, which is moving incredibly rapidly. Every day, there are breakthroughs* (e.g., the quick dominance of DeepMind's* StarCraft* II AI), new researches (like on curiosity-driven learning), and new technologies (e.g. faster running AI enabled hardware chips facilitating lighter and less energy consuming computing), making computation cheaper and faster than ever.

On the other hand, there is Enterprise AI, which is undoubtedly moving forward, though perhaps not at the pace the media coverage on AI makes it seem. While the use cases for AI in the enterprise are very promising (from manual process automation to more complex AI systems powering hyper-efficient supply chains or becoming data-powered advisors to humans working in financial institutions), progress is slower than the AI fantasy, the media sells.

For example, there is a real shortage in computer science students, a shortage that is largely responsible for the lack of AI breakthroughs on the enterprise side. The problem is clear to engineers who use AI in the enterprise. But for many engineers, the real problem is finding the right place to start. Some engineers are more interested in developing new algorithms to address certain business problems than they are in solving the hard science of AI.

There is a clear trend of increasing concern as the need for enterprise AI grows and as applications for these AI capabilities emerge: the more AI-intensive an enterprise is, the more is the concern. The reason, concerns arise, is that enterprise AI can involve a lot of different things, and it is quite hard to have an accurate picture of what's actually going on.

AI Trends for 2020 and beyond

- *Rise of the Data Scientists*

  More and more people are waking to the realization that AI and data science are here to stay and stay for at least the next half century. Many high-tech industries are rising in parallel like Blockchain*, Cyber-security*, Fintech*, Genomics*, Gaming*, IoT*, Quantum-Computing* and Robotics* but all these too, are getting disrupted with Artificial Intelligence.

- *More people in technical domains (than in any other field, even non-technical ones)* **are taking up machine learning programs** from myriad learning resources. Some experts opine that as the industry saw the flood of IT professionals in the past three decades, the current one will see a flood of data scientists rising from all nooks and corners of the technology and education worlds. But this time, the competition will be fiercer than ever. So, it is the industry and academia that need to innovate and create a new way of computing with their data because their competition will be way out in front.

  It is viewed, while machine learning will continue to be the king of the hill, it is strongly felt that as people start to use their data for more than mere data marts or aggregations, there will be a real push towards more practical use of the data, and hence the emergence of data science.

Also, as more companies use data to better understand their customers' needs, it is seen, this is growing in importance and usage. We need to get more people working in this space.

- Explainable* AI, Trust, Ethics, and Bias were the centre stage discussion topics across 2019, the world over. ***In 2020, the pressure will be on making Explainable AI – ethical, unbiased, and trusted.*** The question of ethics and bias is an important one. It is not held that the general human population is particularly bad about bias, it is considered most people are fairly moral in a wide variety of ways, but it will be impossible for the future to be truly ethical or fair unless there is a set of ethical methods for making decisions that are acceptable to everyone.

- ***Worldwide spending on AI systems*** was forecasted to reach $35.8 billion in 2019, an increase of 44% over 2018, and to more than double to $79.2 billion in 2022 as per IDC*, Worldwide Artificial Intelligence Spending Guide.

- ***Many workshops are being organised, participated and attended*** by large enterprises for various business heads of their different business units across the countries on the premise that data leadership needs to be developed at the top levels first and this leadership then helps in percolating down the culture to bottom layers in their respective business units.

- ***With data sets getting better, AI will be able to consider multiple objectives at a faster speed and accuracy*** against the single objective optimization that it currently does.

- ***Machine Learning is becoming mainstream*** for all technology learners and increasingly for non-technical professionals as well.

- ***AI will increasingly be monitoring and refining business processes:*** Several different kinds of AI tools are being developed increasingly by developers worldwide which are making lives of people in various departments easy, fast and effective. These, in turn, are helping humans in refining processes and taking their businesses to the next level.

  AI's role in society is expected to grow exponentially and that will lead to a new paradigm of business innovation. AI is set to play a key role in the economy and will significantly change the way we work. Many things will be automated in the future. But the most important thing is our ability to take advantage of all this automation.

  The human factor will continue to play a crucial role in ensuring that our companies and organizations are successful. A great deal of work is still needed to ensure that we manage the transition to automation more effectively, and this requires a strong, collaborative, and flexible approach from the government and the business world.

- Tech giants and academic researchers are ***working on new algorithms to shrink existing deep-learning models*** without losing their capabilities. Meanwhile, an emerging generation of specialized AI chips promises to pack more computational power into tighter physical spaces, and train and run AI on far less energy.

  One of the biggest surprises was, for decades, we couldn't run deep learning on modern computer hardware, the way most people train a classifier today. The reason is that deep learning uses a lot of the computing power available today of a high-end, mid-range PC. It is worthy to note that now new deep-learning models can work on chips that are similar to a smartphone.

- ***More devices will run AI-powered technology:*** As the next decade approaches and the cost of hardware and software continues to fall, AI tools will increasingly be embedded into our vehicles, household appliances, and workplace tools.

One may be excited now about the possibilities here. We can use data analytics and artificial intelligence to improve the efficiency of car engines and power trains and these will be able to learn to be more efficient, since the more they are exposed to the data, the smarter they become.

Of course, autonomous vehicles aren't the only tools that AI can help us with. If we can create AI systems that perform certain tasks better than us humans, they could be a huge boon for us as well. But we will have to be very careful.

Some of us might be worried about the potential for AI to control us, but at the same time, let us have faith in human ability to prevent this from happening. And, we should all be glad that the tech behind autonomous cars can help us achieve a healthier and more compassionate society.

- *AI increasingly at the 'edge'.* Much of the AI we're used to interacting with now in our day-to-day lives takes place 'in the cloud' – when we search on Google or flick through recommendations on Netflix*, the complex, data-driven algorithms run on high-powered processors inside remote data-centres, with the devices in our hands or on our desktops simply acting as conduits for information to pass through. Increasingly, however, as these algorithms become more efficient and capable of running on low-power devices, AI is taking place at the 'edge,' close to the point where data is gathered and used. This paradigm will continue to become more popular in 2020 and beyond, making AI-powered insights a reality outside of the times and places where super-fast fibre-optic and mobile networks are available. Custom processors designed to carry out real-time analytics on-the-fly will increasingly become part of the technology we interact with day-to-day, and increasingly we will be able to do this even if we have patchy or non-existent internet connections.

- ***AI increasingly is used to create films, music, and games:*** Influence of AI on entertainment media is likely to increase. This year we saw Robert De Niro de-aged in front of our eyes with the assistance of AI, in Martin Scorsese's epic The Irishman, or Microsoft's AI becoming smarter in playing a game by getting trained on a million games played before and such others. The use of AI in creating brand new visual effects and trickery is likely to become increasingly common.

- ***Transparency and Traceability:*** Consumers who are increasingly aware that their personal information is valuable, are demanding control. Many are recognizing the increasing risk of securing and managing personal data. Beyond that, governments in several developed and a few developing countries (including India) are implementing strict legislation to ensure that they do. Transparency and traceability are critical elements to support these digital ethics and privacy needs.

As many more organizations deploy AI and take advantage of machine learning to make decisions in place of humans, this is a further cause for concern. There is a driving need for explainable AI and AI governance. This trend requires a focus on the key elements of trust - integrity, openness, accountability, competence, and consistency.

- ***AI will become ever more present in cybersecurity:*** As hacking*, phishing* and social-engineering-attacks* become ever-more sophisticated, and themselves powered by AI and advanced prediction algorithms, smart technology will play an increasingly important role in protecting us from these attempted intrusions into our lives. AI can be used to spot giveaway signs that digital activity or transactions follow patterns that are likely to be indicators of nefarious activity and raise alarms before defences can be breached and sensitive data compromised.

- As **complementary technologies** such as AI and the IoT **begin to integrate**, Blockchain will see tremendous growth in the enterprises.

- **Human Augmentation*:** Human augmentation explores how technology can be used to deliver cognitive and physical improvements as an integral part of the human experience. It is leveraging technology to increase human capabilities both physically and cognitively. Companies like Boston Dynamics* have already developed a wide variety of human augmenting devices that can be used in factories or on the battlefield.

- **AI will recognize us, even if we don't recognize it:** Perhaps even more unsettlingly, the rollout of facial recognition technology is only likely to intensify as we move into the next decade. Not just in China (where the government is looking at ways of making facial recognition compulsory for accessing services like communication networks and public transport) but around the world, corporations and governments are increasingly investing in these methods of telling who we are and interpreting our activity and behavior.

- **Establishing a better medical environment for patients.** Generally, governments and authorities around the world have developed and implemented laws and regulations to establish a better medical environment for patients. The current medical system still has many shortcomings, including uneven distribution of senior clinicians, high rate of misdiagnosis by primary clinicians, long training period for clinicians, shortage of clinicians in undeveloped areas, and high medical expenses for patients. We may witness overcoming of some of such shortcomings in near future with the help of AI deployment in the medical systems.

However, with the development and advancement of machine learning technology in recent years, AI has gradually changed from theory to practicality. The multiple applications of AI in medicine (warning signals, clinical diagnostics, prevention of diseases, treatment-resumes, and follow-up i.e. convalescence and rehabilitation, etc.) are being proven. Additionally, AI technology has become an important factor that may influence the development of the medical industry and may improve the level of medical services.

Canadian artificial intelligence firm BlueDot was in the news in recent months for warning about the new corona-virus days ahead of the official alerts from the Centre for Disease Control and Prevention* and the World Health Organization. The company was able to do this by tapping different sources of information beyond official statistics about the number of cases reported.

BlueDot's AI algorithm, a type of computer program that improves as it processes more data, brings together news stories in dozens of languages, reports from plant and animal disease tracking networks and airline ticketing data. The result is an algorithm that is better at simulating disease spread than algorithms that rely on public health data.

AI has several applications in the medical field:

1. Greater speed of diagnosis and treatment as compared to previously available tools. And greater precision as compared to conventional methods of assessment.

2. Prevention and treatment of diseases.

3. Assess the condition of patients in clinical settings and accurately diagnose and prepare patients for impending therapy before it begins.

4. Generating predictive models of an individual patient's likelihood of heart attack based on health history.

5. Prescribing the optimal therapeutic options.

6. Providing patient support and increasing comfort for patients.

7. Able to match very high-quality human decision making at the clinical decision-making stage to several different outcomes and situations.

8. Quicker confirmation of medical diagnoses, thus maximizing patient safety.

9. Increased quality as compared to routine or evidence-based medicine (EBM) in general practice.

10. Lower cost, allowing for improvements in providing primary health care services.

Glossary

.csv is a 'comma-separated values' text file that uses a comma to separate values. Each line of the file is a data record. Each record consists of one or more fields, separated by commas. The use of the comma as a field separator is the source of the name for this file format.

.xlsx and XLS files are Microsoft Excel Spreadsheets commonly used to store financial data and to create mathematical models.

Agility means ability to move quickly and easily. It also relates to or denotes a method of project management, used especially for software development, that is characterized by the division of tasks into short phases of work and frequent reassessment and adaptation of plans.

AI is a wide-ranging branch of computer science concerned with building smart machines capable of performing tasks that typically require human intelligence.

AI adoption journey passes through an automation process that goes from deterministic functions moving to the predictive and then to the cognitive stage. Deterministic is centred on automation of repetitive processes to improve productivity. This is the gateway to full-fledged AI adoption. (Deterministic → predictive → cognitive)

AI bias is an inclination or prejudice for or against one person or group, especially in a way considered to be unfair.

AI-friendly datasets are an integral part of the field of machine learning. Major advances in this field can result from advances in learning algorithms (such as deep learning), computer hardware, and, less-intuitively, the availability of high-quality training datasets. High-quality labelled training datasets for supervised and semi-supervised machine learning algorithms are usually difficult and expensive to produce because of the large amount of time needed to label the data.

Algorithm is a finite sequence of well-defined, computer-implementable instructions, typically to solve a class of problems or to perform a computation.

Alphabet is an American multinational company headquartered in Mountain View, California. Alphabet is the world's fourth-largest technology company by revenue and one of the world's most valuable companies.

Amazon is an American multinational technology company based in Seattle, USA with 750,000 employees. It focuses on e-commerce, cloud computing, digital streaming, and artificial intelligence. It is considered one of the Big Four technology companies, along with Google, Apple, and Facebook.

Amazon echo is a new smart speaker product from Amazon that combines voice recognition 'intelligent assistant' capabilities with speaker functionality in a cylindrical speaker form factor.

Amazon's recommendation engine currently uses item-to-item collaborative filtering, which scales to massive data sets and produces high-quality recommendations in real time. This type of filtering matches each of the user's purchased and rated items to similar items, then combines those similar items into a recommendation list for the user.

Analytics managers are business professionals who use their technical skills, industry understanding and knowledge of customers to prepare and present information for decision making. They spend most of their time extracting and translating raw data into meaningful information.

API is an application programming interface. It is a computing interface to a software component or a system, that defines how other components or systems can use it.

Apple is an American multinational technology company headquartered in Cupertino, California (USA), that designs, develops, and sells consumer electronics, computer software, and online services. It is considered one of the Big Five technology companies, alongside Microsoft, Amazon, Google, and Facebook.

Augmented reality is the result of using technology to superimpose information — sounds, images, and text — on the world we see. E.g. T.V. commercials.

Bigdata is a combination of structured and unstructured *data* collected by organizations that can be mined for information and used in machine learning projects, predictive modelling, and other advanced analytics applications.

Blue Dot is a Canadian software company.

Boston Dynamics is an American engineering and robotics design company founded in 1992 as a spin-off from the Massachusetts Institute of Technology (MIT). Headquartered in Waltham, Massachusetts (USA), Boston Dynamics is a wholly owned subsidiary of the Japanese conglomerate SoftBank Group. The company is a pioneer in the field of robotics and is one of the most advanced in its domain.

Breakthrough is a sudden, dramatic, and important discovery or development.

Blockchain, originally Block Chain, is a growing list of records, called blocks, that are linked using cryptography. It is an open, distributed ledger that can record transactions between two parties efficiently and in a verifiable and permanent way.

Bots (short for 'robots') is an automated program that runs over the Internet. Some *bots* run automatically, while others only execute commands when they receive specific input.

Breakout is an arcade game developed and published by Atari, Inc., and released on May 13, 1976.

Business Intelligence (BI) refers to technologies, applications and practices for the collection, integration, analysis, and presentation of business information.

Capabilities development encompasses the traditional scope of professional development (skills-based training, knowledge-based education, and experience), but also incorporates other aspects such as relationships, mandate and direction, tools and work environment, time, motivation and the previously acquired knowledge.

Centre of Excellence (CoE) is a team, a shared facility or an entity that provides leadership, best practices, research, support and/ or training for a focus area. The focus area might be a technology (e.g. Java), a business concept (e.g. Business Process Management - BPM), a skill (e.g. negotiation) or a broad area of study (e.g. Artificial Intelligence, Women's Health, Labourer's Welfare etc.).

Centre for Disease Control and Prevention is a federal government body that protects the health and safety of people at home and abroad through health promotion, prevention and control of disease and injury, public health workforce development & training, and preparedness for new health threats.

CEO – Chief Executive Officer is the highest-ranking executive in a company, whose primary responsibilities include making major corporate decisions, managing the overall operations and resources of a company, acting as the main point of communication between the board of directors (the board) and corporate operations. A CEO is elected by the board and its shareholders and is the public face of the company.

CFO – Chief Financial Officer is the senior executive responsible for managing the financial actions of a company. The CFO's duties include tracking cash flow and financial planning as well as analysing the company's financial strengths and weaknesses and proposing corrective actions.

Clean data is produced by data cleaning process of detecting and correcting (or removing) corrupt or inaccurate records from a record set, table, or database and refers to identifying incomplete, incorrect, inaccurate or irrelevant parts of the data and then replacing, modifying, or deleting the dirty or coarse data.

Cloud infrastructure refers to the hardware and software components – such as servers, storage, a network and virtualization software – that are needed to support the computing requirements of a cloud computing model.

COCO dataset is formatted in JSON and is a collection of 'info', 'licenses', 'images', 'annotations', 'categories' (in most cases), and 'segment info' (in one case).

Cognitive means relating to the mental processes involved in knowing, learning, and understanding things, which are the natural functions of human intelligence as well as that of artificial intelligence.

Cognitive technologies are products of the field of artificial intelligence. They can perform tasks that only humans are able to do. Examples of cognitive technologies include computer vision, machine learning, natural language processing, speech recognition, and robotics.

Content distribution is the act of promoting content to online audiences in multiple media formats through various channels.

COO – Chief Operating Officer is the corporate executive who oversees ongoing business operations within the company. The COO reports to the CEO and is usually second-in-command within the company. Alternative titles for the COO include Chief Operations Officer, Operations Director and Director of Operations.

C-suite refers to the executive-level managers within a company. Common *c-suite* executives include chief executive officer (CEO), chief financial officer (CFO), chief operating officer (COO), and chief information officer (CIO).

CTO – Chief Technology Officer sometimes known as a chief technical officer or chief technologist, is an executive-level position in a company or other establishment whose occupation is focused on the scientific and technological issues within the organization.

Customer data sensitivity relates to sensitive data which is information that must be protected against unauthorized access. The loss, misuse, modification, or unauthorized access to your most sensitive data can damage your business, ruin customer trust and/ or breach customer privacy.

Customer Relationship Management (CRM) is a technology for managing all your company's relationships and interactions with customers and potential customers. The goal is simple: Improve business relationships. A CRM system helps companies stay connected to customers, streamline processes, and improve profitability.

Cyber-security is the practice of defending computers, servers, mobile devices, electronic systems, networks, and data from malicious attacks.

Data analyst translates numbers into plain English. Every business collects data, whether it is sales figures, market research, logistics, or transportation costs. A data analyst's job is to take that data and use it to help companies make better business decisions.

Data architect is a practitioner of data architecture, a data management discipline concerned with designing, creating, deploying, and managing an organization's data architecture.

Data architecture, in part, describes the data structures used by a business and its computer applications software. Essential to realizing the target state, Data Architecture describes how data is processed, stored, and utilized in an information system.

Data engineer is a worker whose primary job responsibility involves preparing data for analytical or operational uses. To carry out their duties, data engineers can be expected to have skills in such programming languages as C#, Java, Python, Ruby, Scala, and SQL.

Data fallacies myths and traps that lie within data. They ultimately lead us to draw incorrect conclusions from data and make poor decisions.

Data formatting is the organization of information according to pre-set specifications.

Data Science (DS) is an inter-disciplinary field that uses scientific methods, processes, algorithms, and systems to extract knowledge and insights from many structured and unstructured data.

Data scientist is someone who knows how to extract meaning from and interpret data, which requires both tools and methods from 'statistics' and 'machine learning', as well as his natural 'human intelligence'. S/he spends a lot of time in the process of collecting, cleaning, and munging data, because data is never clean.

Data set is a collection of data. In the case of tabular data, a data set corresponds to one or more database tables, where every column of a table represents a variable, and each row corresponds to a given record of the data set in question.

Deep Learning (DL) is part of a broader family of machine learning methods based on artificial neural networks.

DeepMind Technologies is a UK artificial intelligence company founded in September 2010 and acquired by Google in 2014. The company is based in London, with research centres in Canada, France, and the United States. In 2015, it became a wholly owned subsidiary of Alphabet Inc.

Deployment is implementation.

Diabetic retinopathy is a complication of diabetes that affects the eyes. It is caused by damage to the blood vessels of the light-sensitive tissue at the back of the eye (retina).

Dirty data refers to data that contains erroneous information. Duplicate data. incorrect data and inaccurate data are all its examples.

Disruptive technology is an innovation that significantly alters the way that consumers, industries, or businesses operate. First steam engine, then electricity, then computers and now artificial intelligence and the likes have been potent disruptive technologies.

DNA or deoxyribonucleic acid is a self-replicating material which is present in nearly all living organisms inside their cells/ nucleus as the main constituent of chromosomes. It is the carrier of genetic information.

Elon Musk (born June 28, 1971) is an engineer, industrial designer, and technology entrepreneur. He is a citizen of South Africa, the United States, and Canada. He is the founder, CEO and chief engineer/designer of SpaceX, co-founder, CEO and product architect of Tesla, Inc . In December 2016, he was ranked 21st on the Forbes list of The World's Most Powerful People, and was ranked joint-first on the Forbes list of the Most Innovative Leaders of 2019.As of May 2020, he has a net worth of $36.5 billion and is listed by Forbes as the 31st-richest person in the world.

Emotional recognition is the process of identifying human emotions (viz. happiness, sadness, disgust, fear, anger, and surprise). As per the scientific study, there are at least 27 different human emotions. People vary widely in their accuracy at recognizing the emotions of others. Use of technology to help people with emotion recognition is a relatively nascent research area.

Encryption language helps in translation of data into a secret code. Encryption is the most effective way to achieve data security. To read an encrypted file, you must have access to a secret key or password that enables you to open/ decrypt it. Unencrypted data is called plain text; encrypted data is referred to as cipher text.

Enterprise AI is the ability to embed AI methodology — which combines the human capacities for learning, perception, and interaction all at a level of complexity that ultimately supersedes our own abilities — into the very core of an organization's data strategy.

Enterprise transformation can be understood as the fundamental change to the way an organization operates, whether that be moving into a new market or operating in a new way.

Ergo hoc proctor hoc (Latin: "after this, therefore because of this") is an informal fallacy that states: "Since event Y followed event X, event Y must have been caused by event X." It is often shortened simply to post hoc fallacy.

Ethics or moral philosophy is a branch of philosophy that involves systematizing, defending, and recommending concepts of right and wrong conduct.

Explainable AI is a set of tools and frameworks to help you develop interpretable and inclusive machine learning models and deploy them with confidence. With it, one can understand feature attributions in AutoML Tables and *AI* Platform and visually investigate model behavior using the What-If Tool.

Facebook is an American online social media and social networking service based in Menlo Park, California (USA) and a flagship service of the namesake company Facebook, Inc. It was founded by Mark Zuckerberg, along with fellow Harvard College students and roommates Eduardo Saverin, Andrew McCollum, Dustin Moskovitz, and Chris Hughes.

File format is a standard way that information is encoded for storage in a computer file. It specifies how bits are used to encode information in a digital storage medium. Some file formats are designed for very particular types of data: PNG files, for example, store bitmapped images using lossless data compression.

Fintech or Financial technologies originally are computer programs and other technologies used to support or enable banking and financial services.

Format consistency refers to the way we choose to present text. Typically, we can modify font type, text size and style. We can also modify the appearance of paragraphs in terms of line spacing and justification.

Fourth Industrial Revolution (IR): 1st. (1780-1870) – Steam Engine| 2nd. (1870-1960) - Electricity| 3rd. (1960-2010) – Computers |4th. (2010 – today) – Connected world.

Gaming is the running of specialized applications known as electronic games or video games on game consoles like X-box and Playstation or on personal computers (in which case the activity is known as online gaming).

Genomics technologies are transforming healthcare with the facility to sequence more genes in shorter time periods and at ever reducing costs.

GitHub brings together the world's largest community of developers to discover, share, and build better software. Presently, more than 2.9M businesses and organisations are using GitHub.

Go is an abstract strategy board game for two players, in which the aim is to surround more territory than the opponent. The players take turns placing the stones on the vacant intersections ('points') of a board. Once placed on the board, stones may not be moved, but stones are removed from the board if 'captured'.

Google is an American multinational technology company that specializes in Internet-related services and products, which include online advertising technologies, a search engine, cloud computing, software, and hardware. It is considered one of the Big Four technology companies alongside Amazon, Apple, and Facebook.

Google Duplex is an artificial intelligence (AI) chat agent that can carry out specific verbal tasks, such as making a reservation or appointment, over the phone.

Google search engine also referred to as Google Web Search or simply Google, is a web search engine developed by Google. It is the most used search engine on the World Wide Web across all platforms handling more than 5 billion searches each day.

Hacking is identifying weakness in computer systems or networks to exploit its weaknesses to gain access.

HCI - is a multidisciplinary field of study focusing on the design of computer technology and the interaction between humans (the users) and computers. While initially concerned with computers, **HCI** has since expanded to cover almost all forms of information technology design.

Histopathologists are doctors who diagnose and study disease using expert medical interpretation of cells and tissue samples. Histopathology is integral to cancer management through staging and grading of tumours and determines the cause of death by performing autopsies.

Human augmentation is generally used to refer to technologies that enhance human productivity or capability, or that somehow add to the human body.

Human genetic disorders are a group of health problems caused by one or more abnormalities in the genome. E.g. cystic fibrosis, sickle cell disease, phenylketonuria, thalassaemia(s), and polycystic kidney disease, etc.

IBM or International Business Machines Corporation is an American multinational technology company headquartered in Armonk, New York (USA), with operations in over 170 countries. IBM produces and sells computer hardware, middleware, and software, and provides hosting and consulting services in areas ranging from mainframe computers to nanotechnology.

IDC or **International Data Corporation** is the premier global provider of market intelligence, advisory services, and events for the information technology industry.

Insight is an accurate and deep understanding.

Internet Explorer (IE) is a World Wide Web browser that comes bundled with the Microsoft Windows operating system (OS). The browser was deprecated in Windows 10 in favour of Microsoft's new Edge Browser. It remains a part of the operating system even though it is no longer the default browser.

IoT or Internet of Things is a system of interrelated computing devices, mechanical and digital machines, objects, animals or people that are provided with unique identifiers (UIDs) and the ability to transfer data over a network without requiring human-to-human or human-to-computer interaction.

Jeopardy is an American television game show created by Merv Griffin. The show features a quiz competition in which contestants are presented with general knowledge clues in the form of answers and must phrase their responses in the form of questions.

JSON or JavaScript Object Notation, is a minimal, readable format for structuring data. It is used primarily to transmit data between a server and web application.

Legacy refers to old/ traditional.

Machine Learning (ML) is the study of computer algorithms that improve automatically through experience.

Microsoft is an American multinational technology company with headquarters in Redmond, Washington (USA). It develops, manufactures, licenses, supports, and sells computer software, consumer electronics, personal computers, and related services. Its best-known software products are the Microsoft Windows line of operating systems, the Microsoft Office suite, and the Internet Explorer.

Monetisation refers to the action or process of earning revenue from an asset, business, etc.

NASDAQ is an American stock exchange located at One Liberty Plaza in New York City (USA). It is ranked second on the list of stock exchanges by market capitalization of shares traded, behind only the New York Stock Exchange (NYSE).

Netflix is an American media-services provider and production company headquartered in Los Gatos, California (USA) and provides online on-demand video entertainment services.

NIKI is an artificial intelligence enabled chat-bot company headquartered in Bangalore, Karnataka

NLP (Natural Language Processing) is a subfield of linguistics, computer science, information engineering, and artificial intelligence concerned with the interactions between computers and human (natural) languages, in particular how to program computers to process and analyse large amounts of natural language data.

Phishing the fraudulent practice of sending emails purporting to be from reputable companies in order to induce individuals to reveal personal information, such as passwords and credit card numbers.

Predictive analytics encompasses a variety of statistical techniques from data mining, predictive modeling, and machine learning, that analyze current and historical facts to make predictions about future or otherwise unknown events.

Predictive insights are predicted future outcomes and trends extracted from existing data sets.

Predictive maintenance is a technique to predict the future failure point of a machine component, so that the component can be replaced, based on a plan, just before it fails. Thus, equipment downtime is minimized, and the component lifetime is maximized.

Python is a high-level general-purpose programming language.

Quality analyst evaluates products, systems, and software to ensure they are free of defects and meet the quality standards of the organization.

Quantum computing is an area of computing focused on developing computer technology based on the principles of quantum theory, which explains the behaviour of energy and material on the atomic and subatomic levels.

Robotics is the branch of technology that deals with the design, construction, operation, and application of robots.

Robot rights is the concept that people should have moral obligations towards their machines, like 'human rights' or 'animal rights'. These could include the right to life and liberty, freedom of thought and expression and equality before the law.

Role of AI/ML in making decisions in place of humans AI includes the automation of physical and cognitive tasks. It helps people perform tasks faster and better and make better decisions. It enables the automation of decision making without human intervention.

SBEs are small business enterprises.

Security risks can be created by malware, that is, bad software, that can infect your computer, destroy your files, steal your data, or allow an attacker to gain access to your system without your knowledge or authorization. Examples include viruses, worms, ransomware, spyware, and Trojan.

Sine qua non is an essential condition, a thing that is necessary. E.g. 'grammar and usage are sine qua non of language teaching and learning'.

SMEs are small and medium enterprises.

Social commerce is a subset of electronic commerce that involves social media, online media that supports social interaction, and user contributions to assist online buying and selling of products and services. More succinctly, social commerce is the use of social network(s) in the context of e-commerce transactions.

Social engineering attacks typically involve some form of psychological manipulation, fooling otherwise unsuspecting users or employees into handing over confidential or sensitive data. Commonly, social engineering involves email or other communication that invokes urgency, fear, or similar emotions in the victim, leading the victim to promptly reveal sensitive information, click a malicious link, or open a malicious file. Because social engineering involves a human element, preventing these attacks can be tricky for enterprises.

StarCraft II is a military science fiction media franchise that debuted this game in 1998. It has grown to include a number of other games as well as eight novelizations, two Amazing Stories articles, a board game, and other licensed merchandise such as collectible statues and toys.

Statistics is a branch of mathematics that studies methodologies to gather, review, analyse and draw conclusions from data.

Stephen Hawking (1942 – 2018) an English theoretical Physicist and Cosmologist known for his work with black holes and relativity, and the author of popular science books like 'A Brief History of Time', 'A Briefer History of Time', 'Blackholes and Baby Universe', and 'The Universe in a Nutshell', etc.

Super Mario is a series of fantasy platform games created by Nintendo featuring their mascot, Mario. Alternatively called the Super Mario Bros.

The games have simple plots, typically with Mario rescuing the kidnapped Princess Peach from the primary antagonist, Bowser.

Tay was an artificial intelligence chatter bot that was originally released by Microsoft Corporation via Twitter on March 23, 2016; it caused subsequent controversy when the bot began to post inflammatory and offensive tweets through its Twitter account, causing Microsoft to shut down the service only 16 hours after the release.

Telematics is the joining of two sciences—telecommunications, a branch of technology including phone lines and cables, and informatics such as computer systems. Today, the term is commonly used in reference to the telematics solutions utilized in commercial fleet vehicles.

Tractica, an Informa business, is a market intelligence firm that provides in-depth analysis of global market opportunities surrounding human interaction with technology, including qualitative and quantitative assessment of Artificial Intelligence, Robotics, User Interface Technologies, Wearable Devices, and Digital Health.

Troll, is *someone who posts inflammatory, extraneous, or off-topic messages in an online community, such as an online discussion forum, chat room, or blog, with the primary intent of provoking readers into an emotional response or of otherwise disrupting normal on-topic discussion.* While Twitter definitely has people like this engaged in the online social network, these self-involved types of people ultimately, make people collectively groan in disappointment.

van Gogh (Vincent van Gogh), (1853 – 1890) was a Dutch post-impressionist painter who is among the most famous and influential figures in the history of Western art.

Walmart Stores is an American multinational retail corporation that operates a chain of hypermarkets, discount department stores, and grocery stores, headquartered in Bentonville, Arkansas (USA). It is the world's largest company by revenue, with US$ 514.405 billion, according to the Fortune Global 500 list in 2019.

Web analytics is the measurement and analysis of data to inform an understanding of user behaviour across web pages.

Yellow Messenger is Asia's largest Conversational AI platform for enterprises and was founded in 2015.

XML i.e. Extensible Markup Language, is a mark-up language that defines a set of rules for encoding documents in a format that is both human-readable and machine-readable.

.

References

1. https://www.altexsoft.com/blog/datascience/preparing-your-dataset-for-machine-learning-8-basic-techniques-that-make-your-data-better/

2. https://www.businessinsider.com/artificial-intelligence-ai-most-impressive-achievements-2017-3?IR=T

3. www.dataiku.com

4. Deloitte 2018 Cognitive Survey

5. www.Gartner.com

6. MIT Research Report-2017

7. https://medium.com/layer7-ai/the-build-or-buy-decision-in-ai-5302be064364

8. AI & Analytics, Wiley

9. Prediction Machines, Harvard Business Review

10. https://www.sellingpower.com

11. McKinsey, USA

12. www.O'Reilly.com

13. McKinsey Global Institute

14. McKinsey article on Bridging the Gap between Humans and AI

15. Topbots.com

16. https://www.weforum.org/agenda/2016/10/top-10-ethical-issues-in- artificial-intelligence/

17. www.cdotrends.com

18. https://www.forbes.com/sites/bernardmarr/2020/01/06/the-top-10-artificial-intelligence-trends-everyone-should-be-watching-in-2020/#1fc62159390b

19. https://towardsdatascience.com/top-10-technology-trends-for-2020-4a179fdd53b1

20. www.wikipedia.org

Index